More Recipe
Round-ups

Acknowledgements

This book features recipes
taken from the Dairy Diaries
published between 1986 and 1990,
together with others selected
from the
Milk Marketing Board archives.

Designed by AMBA Designs

Edited by Sheelagh Donovan

Production John Vanner

Printed by Jarrold Printing, Norwich.

© Milk Marque 1995

More Recipe Round-ups

A SELECTION OF
POPULAR RECIPES FROM
DAIRY DIARIES
1986-1990

── Recipe Notes ──

- 1 -
Follow metric or imperial measurements in
the recipe. Do not mix the two.

- 2 -
When measuring milk, can sizes, etc.
exact measurements have been given.
e.g. 568ml (1 pint)

- 3 -
All spoon measures are level.
tsp = teaspoon
tbsp = tablespoon

- 4 -
Cooking times may vary slightly,
depending on individual ovens.
Use the centre shelf in the oven
unless otherwise stated.

CALORIES

The calorie values in this book may differ from those in the original diaries.
This is due to the publication of a revised edition of the
official food tables plus availability of data from food manufacturers and retailers.
Some recipes have also been modified in line with current healthy eating guidelines.
Each recipe has been rounded up or down to the nearest 5 calories.

'Milk' in the recipes has been calculated as whole milk.

'Cheese' in the recipes has been calculated as full fat unless otherwise stated.

F

This symbol indicates the recipe is suitable for freezing.
Some recipes e.g. those with crunchy toppings, have not been given
the freezer symbol as the quality of the dish when reheated,
will not match that of the freshly prepared dish. You may choose to freeze these dishes.

✳ EGGS

The Department of Health advises that the general public should
avoid eating raw eggs or uncooked food/recipes made from them.

There is a pasteurised dried egg white powder available that can be substituted in these recipes.
Follow the manufacturers instructions when reconstituting the powder and make a direct substitution.
Do not be deterred by the gelatine-like odour when the powder is reconstituted.

Contents

285 Calories per portion

Bean Soup   SERVES 4

Flageolet beans - *400g can*
OR *75g (3oz) dried*
Butter - *15g (½ oz)*
Onion - *1 medium, chopped*
Plain wholemeal flour - *15g (½ oz)*
Fresh milk - *750ml (1¼ pint)*
Vegetable stock cube - *1*

Fresh parsley - *15ml (1 tbsp) chopped*
Fresh soured cream - *30ml (2 tbsp)*

METHOD

1 Drain canned beans or cook dried beans according to packet instructions.

2 Melt butter in a saucepan. Gently cook onion until soft. Add flour and cook for 1 minute. Blend in milk and sprinkle in stock cube. Heat, stirring continuously until the soup boils. Add beans and simmer gently for 5 minutes. Check seasoning. Stir in parsley and soured cream before serving.

325 Calories per portion **F**

Corn & Bacon Chowder   SERVES 4

Streaky bacon - *75g (3oz) rinded and chopped*
Onion - *1 medium, chopped*
Potatoes - *450g (1 lb) peeled and diced*
Frozen sweetcorn - *225g (8oz)*
Chicken stock - *450ml (¾ pint)*
Fresh milk - *450ml (¾ pint)*
Fresh parsley - *chopped, to serve*

METHOD

1 Cook bacon lightly in a non stick saucepan for 2 minutes. Drain well.

2 Add onion, potatoes, sweetcorn and stock. Bring to the boil, cover and simmer for 15 minutes. Cool slightly.

3 Purée half the vegetables and the liquid from the soup in a food processor or blender. Return to the vegetables in the saucepan, add the milk and reheat gently without boiling. Serve sprinkled with parsley.

Soups

320 Calories per portion Ⓕ

Turkey Chowder
SERVES 4

Butter - *25g (1oz)*
Onion - *1, chopped*
Potatoes - *225g (8oz) peeled and diced*
Chicken stock - *300ml (½ pint)*
Bay leaf - *1*
Cooked turkey - *175g (6oz) diced*
Creamed sweetcorn - *298g can*
Fresh milk - *450ml (¾ pint)*

Cornflour - *15ml (1 tbsp)*
Salt *and freshly ground* **black pepper**
Fresh parsley - *30ml (2 tbsp) chopped*

METHOD
1 Melt butter in a large saucepan. Gently cook onion and potatoes for 5 minutes.

2 Add stock, bay leaf and turkey. Simmer for 10 minutes. Add sweetcorn and most of the milk. Simmer for 10 minutes.

3 Blend remaining milk and cornflour. Stir in about 90ml (6tbsp) soup then return to saucepan, stirring continuously. Bring to the boil and simmer for 2 minutes. Season to taste, remove bayleaf and stir in parsley before serving.

290 Calories per portion Ⓕ

Bean & Pasta Soup
SERVES 4

Haricot beans - *75g (3oz)*
Pasta shapes - *50g (2oz)*
Butter - *15g (½ oz)*
Onion - *1 medium, chopped*
Garlic cloves - *2, crushed*
Ripe tomatoes - *4, skinned and de-seeded*
Fresh milk - *750ml (1¼ pint)*
Salt *and freshly ground* **black pepper**

METHOD
1 Cook beans and pasta according to packet instructions. Drain.

2 Melt butter in a large saucepan. Gently cook onion, garlic and tomatoes for 3 minutes. Add milk and simmer for 2 minutes.

3 Purée half the beans and half the milk/tomato mixture in a food processor or blender. Return purée to the saucepan. Add the pasta and remaining beans. Season, reheat gently and serve.

195 Calories per portion

Chilled Cucumber & Coriander Soup SERVE

Cucumber - *1, finely diced*
Low fat natural yogurt - *300g (10oz)*
Fresh single cream - *300ml (½ pint)*
Garlic clove - *1, crushed*
Fresh coriander - *45ml (3 tbsp) chopped*
Fresh mint - *7.5ml (½ tbsp) chopped*
Salt *and freshly ground* **black pepper**
Cucumber and yellow pepper - *chopped, to garnish*

METHOD

1 Place cucumber, yogurt, cream and garlic in a food processor or blender. Blend until nearly smooth.

2 Stir in coriander and mint. Season to taste. Chill for several hours. Check seasoning. Serve garnished with cucumber and yellow pepper.

175 Calories per portion

Chilled Lettuce Soup SERVES 4

Lettuce leaves - *225g (8oz), washed*
Butter - *25g (1 oz)*
Onion - *1 medium, chopped*
Plain flour - *25g (1 oz)*
Chicken stock - *300ml (½ pint)*
Salt *and freshly ground* **black pepper**
Nutmeg - *pinch, freshly grated*
Fresh milk - *450ml (¾ pint)*
Croûtons - *to garnish*

METHOD

1 Shred lettuce. Blanch in boiling water for 1 minute. Drain, rinse under cold running water. Drain again.

2 Melt butter in a large saucepan. Add onion and gently cook until soft. Add flour and cook for 1 minute. Add stock, most of the lettuce, seasoning and nutmeg. Bring to the boil. Cool slightly.

3 Purée in a food processor or blender. Add milk then cool quickly by stirring soup, while standing saucepan in a bowl of cold water. Add remaining lettuce. Chill for several hours before serving, garnished with croûtons.

Soups

200 Calories per portion (F)

Cream of Cauliflower Soup

SERVES 4

Cauliflower - *½*
Butter - *15g (½ oz)*
Onion - *1 small, chopped*
Fresh milk - *750ml (1¼ pint)*
Chicken stock cube - *1*
Nutmeg - *2.5ml (½ tsp) freshly grated*

Celery salt - *to season*
Black pepper - *freshly ground*
Fresh parsley and croûtons - *to garnish*

METHOD

1 Break cauliflower into florets.

2 Melt butter in a large saucepan. Add florets and onion and cook gently for 2 minutes.

3 Add milk, stock cube, nutmeg and seasoning. Bring to boil, cover and simmer for 10 minutes. Cool slightly and purée in a food processor or blender. Reheat gently and serve garnished with parsley and croûtons.

---

145 Calories per portion (F)

Courgette & Cumin Soup

SERVES 4

Courgettes - *350g (12oz)*
Butter - *15g (½ oz)*
Onion - *1 medium, chopped*
Garlic clove - *1, crushed*
Ground cumin - *5ml (1 tsp)*
Potatoes - *150g (5 oz) peeled and cubed*

Salt *and freshly ground* **black pepper**
Chicken stock - *450ml (¾ pint)*
Fresh milk - *300ml (½ pint)*

METHOD

1 Thickly slice most of the courgettes, reserving a few thin slices for garnish.

2 Melt butter in a large saucepan. Gently cook onion and garlic for 5 minutes. Add cumin, cook for 1 minute. Add potatoes and courgettes, season and cook for 2 minutes.

3 Add stock and milk, bring to boil, cover and simmer for 15 minutes.

4 Purée in a food processor or blender and serve hot or chilled, garnished with courgette slices.

125 Calories per portion Ⓕ

Parsley Soup SERVES 4

Fresh parsley - *100g (4oz) chopped*
Onion - *1 small, chopped*
Potato - *1 medium, peeled and diced*
Garlic clove - *1, crushed*
Chicken stock - *450ml (¾ pint)*
Cornflour - *25g (1 oz)*

Fresh milk - *300ml (½ pint)*
Salt *and freshly ground* **black pepper**

METHOD

1 Place parsley, onion, potato, garlic and stock in a large saucepan. Bring to boil and simmer for 20 minutes. Cool slightly. Purée in a processor or blender. Return to rinsed saucepan.

2 Blend cornflour with a little milk. Add to soup with the remaining milk and bring to boil, stirring. Cook for 2 minutes. Serve hot or chilled.

260 Calories per portion

Chicken Soup SERVES 4

Chicken breast - *250g (8oz) raw*
Fresh tarragon - *10ml (2 tsp) chopped*
Lemon - *1, grated rind only*
Salt *and freshly ground* **black pepper**
Egg white - *1 (size 3)*
Butter - *15g (½ oz)*
Plain flour - *25g (1 oz)*
Fresh milk - *900ml (1½ pints)*

Chicken stock cube - *1*
Watercress - *½ bunch, to garnish*

METHOD

1 Mince chicken. Beat in tarragon, lemon rind, seasoning and egg white. Roll into small balls.

2 Place butter, flour and milk in a saucepan. Crumble in stock cube and bring to the boil, stirring continuously. Season lightly with pepper.

3 Add chicken balls then simmer for 5 minutes, adding shredded watercress just before serving.

205 Calories per portion **F**

Guy's Pumpkin Soup

SERVES 4

Pumpkin - *900g (2 lb) peeled, seeded and chopped*
Onion - *1 medium, chopped*
Turmeric - *2.5ml (½ tsp)*
Chopped tomatoes - *100g (4oz) canned*
Sugar - *5ml (1 tsp)*
Nutmeg - *pinch, freshly grated*
Fresh milk - *568ml (1 pint)*
Cornflour - *10ml (2 tsp)*
Low fat natural yogurt - *300g (10oz)*
Chopped parsley and yogurt - *to serve*

METHOD

1 Place pumpkin, onion, turmeric, tomatoes,
sugar, nutmeg and milk in a large saucepan.
Bring to boil, cover and simmer for 15-20 minutes.
Cool and purée in a processor or blender. Return
to rinsed saucepan.

2 Blend cornflour and a little yogurt. Add to the
soup with the remaining yogurt. Bring to
simmering point but do not boil. Serve garnished
with parsley and a swirl of yogurt.

240 Calories per portion **F**

Crab Soup

SERVES 4

Easy cook brown rice - *100g (4oz)*
Fresh milk - *300ml (½ pint)*
Crab meat - *100g (4oz)*
Vegetable stock - *568ml (1 pint)*
Anchovy essence - *10ml (2 tsp)*
Fresh single cream - *150ml (¼ pint)*
Lemon juice - *15ml (1 tbsp)*
Paprika and tomato roses - *to garnish*
Japanese rice crackers - *to serve*

METHOD

1 Place rice and milk in a large saucepan.
Bring to boil and simmer for 20 minutes.

2 Add crab, stock, essence, cream and lemon juice.
Bring gently to the boil. Serve, garnished with paprika
and a tomato rose and accompanied with rice crackers.

Soups

250 Calories per portion Ⓕ

Parsnip & Carrot Soup SERVES 4

Onion - *1, medium, chopped*
Parsnips - *350g (12oz) peeled and diced*
Carrots - *350g (12oz) peeled and diced*
Vegetable stock - *568ml (1 pint)*
Peanut butter - *45ml (3 tbsp)*
Fresh milk - *568ml (1 pint)*
Low fat natural yogurt - *to serve*
Chopped parsley - *to serve*

METHOD

1 Place vegetables in a large saucepan with the stock and peanut butter. Bring to boil, cover and simmer for 15 minutes.

2 Purée half the soup in a processor or blender. Return to the saucepan add milk and reheat gently. Serve with a swirl of yogurt and parsley.

---

435 Calories per portion

Five Bean Soup SERVES 6

Red kidney beans - *75g (3oz)*
Haricot beans - *75g (3oz)*
Pinto beans - *75g (3oz)*
Black eye beans - *75g (3oz)*
Flageolet beans - *75g (3oz)*
Ham stock cubes - *2*
Celery - *2 sticks*
Carrots - *1 medium, halved*
Onion - *200g (7oz), studded with cloves*

Tomatoes - *225g (8oz), skinned and chopped*
Black pepper *freshly ground*
Onion - *200g (7oz)*
Garlic - *1 clove, crushed*
Butter - *25g (1 oz)*
French bread - *12 slices, toasted*
English Mozzarella - *100g (4oz) sliced*

METHOD

1 Blanch beans, apart from flageolet beans for 1 minute. Drain. Put blanched beans in a large saucepan. Add stock cubes dissolved in 2 litres (3½ pints) water. Add celery, carrot and onion. Bring to the boil and simmer for about 3 hours or until beans are tender. Add flageolet beans after an hour of cooking.

2 Remove vegetables, add tomatoes and check seasoning. Reheat without boiling.

3 Finely chop onion. Melt butter in a saucepan. Gently cook onion and garlic until soft. Season. Spread on toasted bread, top with Mozzarella and grill until golden. Float on soup to serve.

265 Calories per portion

Vegetable Chowder SERVES 4

Wholemeal macaroni - *100g (4oz)*
Butter - *25g (1 oz)*
Onion - *175g (6oz) sliced*
Carrot - *225g (8oz) diced*
Celery - *3 sticks, sliced*
Salt *and freshly ground* **black pepper**
Tomatoes - *397g can*
Vegetable stock - *300ml (½ pint)*
Bay leaf - *1*
Dried oregano - *5ml (1 tsp)*
Fresh milk - *300ml (½ pint)*
Fresh parsley - *to garnish*

METHOD

1 Cook macaroni as directed on the packet. Drain.

2 Melt butter in a large saucepan. Gently fry onion, carrot and celery for several minutes. Season.

3 Add tomatoes with juice, stock, bay leaf and oregano. Cover and simmer until vegetables are tender. Stir in macaroni and milk and reheat without boiling. Serve sprinkled with parsley.

---

265 Calories per portion Ⓕ

Coconut Soup SERVES 4

Butter - *25g (1 oz)*
Onions - *2 large, sliced*
Plain flour - *15g (½ oz)*
Fresh milk - *750ml (1¼ pint)*
Desiccated coconut - *30ml (2 tbsp)*
Eating apple - *1, peeled, cored and sliced*
English Cheddar cheese - *50g (2oz) grated*

METHOD

1 Melt butter in a large saucepan. Add onions and cook gently until soft. Stir in flour and cook for 1 minute.

2 Gradually stir in milk and coconut and bring to boil, stirring. Add apple, cover and simmer for 30 minutes. Cool slightly and purée in a processor or blender. Return to saucepan and cook for 5 minutes. Serve with grated cheese.

Ⓕ

Herby Cheese Dip with Crûdités

Fresh parsley - *15ml (1 tbsp) chopped*
Fresh mint - *15ml (1 tbsp) chopped*
English Cheddar cheese - *175g (6oz) grated*
Cottage cheese - *75g (3oz)*
Fresh milk - *150ml (¼ pint)*
Garlic clove - *1, crushed*
Salt *and freshly ground* **black pepper**
Corn chips - *to serve*

METHOD
1 Beat herbs and cheeses in a bowl until smooth.
Blend in milk, garlic and seasoning. Chill well
and serve with crûdités and corn chips.

CRÛDITÉS
Carrot sticks
Cucumber sticks
Celery sticks
Cauliflower florets
Radishes

Avocado Dip   SERVES 4-6

Avocado - *1*
Fresh lime or lemon juice - *15ml (1 tbsp)*
Medium fat curd cheese - *225g (8oz)*
Black pepper *freshly ground*
Garlic cloves - *2, crushed*
Hot pepper sauce - *10 drops*
Raw vegetables - *cut into sticks, to serve*

METHOD
1 Peel avocado and discard the stone. Cut 2 slices for
garnish and brush with a little lime juice to retain the
colour.

2 Mash remaining avocado, lime juice and curd
cheese until smooth. Blend in pepper, garlic
and pepper sauce. Cover and chill. Garnish
with avocado slices and serve with raw
vegetables.

310 Calories per portion (F)

Lancashire Mushroom Rolls SERVES 4

Butter - *20g (¾ oz) + melted for brushing*
Onion - *1 small, finely chopped*
Garlic cloves - *2, crushed*
Button mushrooms - *100g (4oz) chopped*
Wholemeal breadcrumbs - *75g (3oz) freshly grated*
Dried basil - *5ml (1 tsp)*
Lancashire cheese - *100g (4oz) crumbled*
Filo pastry - *8 sheets*

METHOD

1 Melt butter in a saucepan. Gently cook onion and garlic for 2 minutes. Add mushrooms and cook for 2 minutes, stirring. Remove from heat and stir in breadcrumbs, basil and cheese.

2 Brush half each sheet of pastry with melted butter. Fold in half lengthwise. Divide filling between the sheets, not quite reaching the edges, fold edges in and roll up.

3 Place on a greased baking sheet, brush with melted butter and bake at 190°C (375°F), mark 5 for 20 minutes until golden. Serve hot.

Blue Cheese & Poppy Dip SERVES 4-6

Blue Stilton - *150g (5oz) crumbled*
Cottage cheese - *175g (6oz)*
Low fat natural yogurt - *150g (5oz)*
Reduced calorie mayonnaise - *30ml (2 tbsp)*
Poppy seeds - *15ml (1 tbsp) + extra to garnish*

METHOD

1 Mix ingredients together well. Spoon into serving dish and chill for several hours. Garnish with extra poppy seeds and serve with sticks of raw vegetables.

Spicy Dip SERVES 4-6

Low fat curd cheese - *225g (8oz)*
Low fat hazelnut yogurt - *150g (5oz)*
Low fat natural yogurt - *150g (5oz)*
Mild chilli powder - *2.5ml (½ tsp)*
Fresh parsley - *10ml (2 tsp) chopped*
Chopped hazelnuts and parsley - *to garnish*

METHOD

1 Beat all ingredients until smooth. Spoon into serving dish and chill. Serve garnished with nuts and parsley.

Starters

220 Calories per portion

Cheese Mousse SERVES 4

White Cheshire cheese - *50g (2oz) grated*
English mustard - *5ml (1 tsp)*
Nutmeg - *large pinch, freshly grated*
Fresh double cream - *150ml (¼ pint)*
Egg white* - *1 (size 3) whisked*
Lemon slices and parsley - *to garnish*
*See page 2

METHOD

1 Beat cheese, mustard and nutmeg. Whip cream to form soft peaks and fold into the cheese.

2 Fold in egg white and spoon into 4 ramekins. Chill and serve garnished with lemon and parsley.

60 Calories each

Cottage Tarts MAKES 16

Wholemeal bread - *8 thin slices from large loaf*
Butter - *25-40g (1-1½ oz) melted*
Low fat cottage cheese - *225g (8oz)*
Red pepper - *1 small, chopped*
Yellow pepper - *1 small, chopped*
Celery sticks - *2, chopped*
Spring onions - *4, finely chopped*
Salt *and freshly ground* **black pepper**
Dried mixed herbs - *5ml (1 tsp)*
Fresh parsley - *15ml (1 tbsp) chopped*

METHOD

1 Using a 7.5cm (3 inch) cutter, cut 2 circles from each slice of bread. Flatten each with a rolling pin then gently press into 16 buttered patty tins. Brush with melted butter and bake at 200°C (400°F), mark 6 for 15 minutes until crisp and golden. Cool.

2 Mix remaining ingredients, saving a little parsley for garnish. Divide between cases and serve.

0 Calories each

Cheesy Profiteroles   MAKES 16

Butter - *50g (2oz)*
Fresh milk - *150ml (¼ pint)*
Plain flour - *75g (3oz) sifted*
Eggs - *2 (size 3) beaten*
Blue Stilton - *25g (1oz) crumbled*
Eggs - *2 (size 3) hard boiled, chopped*
Curry powder - *5ml (1 tsp)*

Fresh parsley - *30ml (2 tbsp) chopped*
Reduced calorie garlic mayonnaise - *30ml (2 tbsp)*

METHOD

Melt butter in milk in a saucepan. Bring to boil then remove from heat. Tip flour into the hot liquid, beating with a wooden spoon until the mixture is smooth and forms ball. Cool slightly.

Vigorously beat in sufficient egg, a little at a time, to give glossy mixture of piping consistency. Blend in the Stilton.

Place teaspoons of mixture on a greased baking sheet. Bake at 200°C (400°F), mark 6 for 15 minutes. Slit to allow steam to escape and cool on a wire rack.

Blend remaining ingredients and spoon into the profiteroles. Serve.

05 Calories per portion

Three Cheese Paté   SERVES 4

Low fat curd cheese - *175g (6oz)*
Lancashire cheese - *100g (4oz) grated*
Red Windsor cheese - *100g (4oz) grated*
Fresh soured cream - *105ml (7 tbsp)*
Fresh chives - *15ml (1 tbsp) chopped*
Fresh coriander or parsley - *15ml (1 tbsp) + a little to garnish*
Black pepper *freshly ground*

METHOD

Blend cheeses together well in a bowl.

Add cream, chives and coriander and beat until smooth. Season with pepper.

Spoon into 4 ramekins and chill. Serve garnished with coriander.

165 Calories per portion **F**

Vegetable Terrine SERVES 6

Butter - *40g (1½ oz)*
Wholemeal flour - *50g (2oz)*
Fresh milk - *300ml (½ pint)*
Salt *and freshly ground* **black pepper**
Frozen peas - *100g (4oz) cooked*

Cauliflower - *½, cooked*
Cottage cheese - *100g (4oz)*
Lancashire cheese - *50g (2oz), crumbled*
Carrots - *2, chopped and cooked*
Onion - *1 small, chopped and cooked*

METHOD

1 Grease and base line a 700g (1½ lb) loaf tin.

2 Place butter, flour and milk in a saucepan. Heat, stirring, until sauce boils. Cook for 2 minutes. Season.

3 Purée peas and one third of sauce in a processor or blender. Pour into tin. Purée cauliflower and cheeses with half the remaining sauce. Pour into tin. Purée carrots, onion and seasoning with remaining sauce. Pour into tin. Smooth the surface and cover with greased greaseproof paper.

4 Stand tin in a roasting tin, half filled with hot water. Bake at 170°C (325°F), mark 3 for 1½ hours. Cool and chill well before serving.

240 Calories per portion **F**

Cucumber Cheesecake SERVES 8

Cucumber - *225g (8oz) peeled and cubed*
Gelatine - *11g sachet*
Low fat curd cheese - *450g (1 lb)*
Fresh soured cream - *300ml (½ pint)*
Salt *and freshly ground* **black pepper**
Spring onions - *6, chopped*
Fresh coriander or parsley - *45ml (3 tbsp) chopped*
Wholemeal crispbreads - *100g (4oz) crushed*
Butter - *50g (2oz) melted*
Lemon and cucumber slices - *to decorate*

METHOD

1 Pat cucumber dry with kitchen towel.

2 Dissolve gelatine as directed on the packet.

3 Blend cheese and cream then fold in cucumber, seasoning, onions, herbs and gelatine. Turn into a lightly oiled 1.1 litre (2 pint) fluted mould. Chill until set.

4 Mix crispbreads and butter and gently press on top of the cheesecake. Chill overnight. Unmould before serving, garnished with lemon and cucumber slices.

175 Calories per portion Ⓕ

Fish & Watercress Ring SERVES 4

Smoked haddock - *350g (12oz) skinned*
Fresh milk - *300ml (½ pint)*
Onion - *1 small, chopped*
Eggs - *2 (size 3)*
Black pepper *freshly ground*
Watercress - *1 bunch, trimmed*
Whole prawns - *to garnish*

METHOD

1 Purée fish, milk, onion, eggs, pepper and half the watercress in a processor or blender. It will be easier in batches, if using a blender.

2 Spoon into a greased 900ml (1½ pint) ring mould, cover with foil and stand in a roasting tin, half filled with hot water. Bake at 170°C (325°F), mark 3 for 1 hour until firm. Invert onto a serving plate and serve hot or cold, garnished with remaining watercress and prawns.

255 Calories per portion

Hot Fish Terrine SERVES 8

Butter - *25g (1 oz)*
Plain flour - *40g (1½ oz)*
Fresh milk - *450ml (¾ pint)*
Smoked cod fillets - *550g (1¼ lb) skinned*
Fresh double cream - *150ml (¼ pint)*
Garlic clove - *1, crushed*

Eggs - *3 (size 3)*
Salt *and freshly ground* **black pepper**
Fresh parsley - *45ml (3 tbsp) chopped*
Peeled prawns - *75g (3oz)*
Parsley and lemon slices - *to garnish*

METHOD

1 Place butter, flour and milk in a saucepan. Heat, stirring, until sauce boils. Cook for 2 minutes.

2 Purée the sauce, fish, cream, garlic, eggs and seasoning in a processor or blender.

3 Spoon half the mixture into a greased, base lined 900g (2 lb) loaf tin. Sprinkle with parsley and most of the prawns. Top with remaining mixture and buttered greaseproof paper.

4 Stand tin in a roasting tin, half filled with hot water. Bake at 150°C (300°F), mark 2 for 2 hours. Turn onto a serving plate, draining off any juices and garnish with prawns, parsley and lemon.

200 Calories per portion

Hot Avocados SERVES 4

Avocados - *2 small*
Lemon juice - *10ml (2 tsp)*
Cottage cheese - *175g (6oz)*
Canned salmon - *50g (2oz) flaked*
Canned sweetcorn - *25g (1 oz)*
Chopped chives - *to garnish*

MICROWAVE INSTRUCTIONS

1 Halve avocados and remove stones. Brush surfaces with lemon juice.

2 Mix cottage cheese, salmon and sweetcorn then spoon into cavities.

3 Place on a plate, thinner ends pointing inwards.
Cook on HIGH for 3 minutes. Serve immediately,
sprinkled with chives.

Timings are for a 600 watt oven.

150 Calories per portion

Santa's Salmon SERVES 4

Medium fat soft cheese - *100g (4oz)*
Fresh soured cream - *60ml (4 tbsp)*
Spring onions - *2, finely chopped*
Ground bay leaves - *pinch*
Black pepper *freshly ground*
Smoked salmon - *100g (4oz) sliced*
Red and green pepper - *to garnish*

METHOD

1 Blend soft cheese, cream, spring onions and
bay leaves. Season with black pepper.

2 Spread mixture over salmon slices and roll up.
Chill. Serve garnished with peppers, cut
into holly leaves and berries.

Starters

124 Calories each

Spiced Samosa Parcels SERVES 6

Plain flour - *50g (2oz)*
Ground cumin - *5ml (1 tsp)*
Egg - *1 (size 3)*
Fresh milk - *150ml (¼ pint)*
Butter - *melted for pancakes*
Lean minced beef - *100g (4oz)*

Onion - *1 small, finely chopped*
Green pepper - *½, deseeded and chopped*
Caraway seeds - *5ml (1 tsp)*
Piccalilli - *15ml (1 tbsp)*
Mango chutney - *15ml (1 tbsp)*
Mung bean sprouts - *50g (2oz)*
Alfalfa sprouts - *30ml (2 tbsp)*

METHOD

1 Sift flour and cumin into a bowl. Beat in egg and milk to form a smooth batter.

2 Use batter to make 6 pancakes as on page 66. Keep warm.

3 Dry fry beef, onion, pepper and caraway seeds for 5 minutes. Drain off excess fat. Add piccalilli and chutney and cook for 10 minutes. Add mung bean and alfalfa sprouts.

4 Place filling in the centre of each pancake. Wrap up to form parcel. Place on an overproof plate, brush with a little butter and grill for 3-4 minutes. Serve immediately.

40 Calories per portion

Turkey Tempura SERVES 4

Plain flour - *150g (5oz)*
Salt - *2.5ml (½ tsp)*
Egg - *1 (size 3) separated*
Fresh milk - *300ml (½ pint)*
Cauliflower - *½, small florets*
Broccoli - *225g (8oz) small florets*
Baby Brussels sprouts - *10*
Carrots - *3, peeled, cut in sticks*
Cooked turkey - *225g (8oz) cut in chunks*
Barbecue sauce - *to serve*

METHOD

1 Mix flour, salt and egg yolk in a bowl. Gradually beat in milk to give a smooth batter. Whisk egg white until stiff and fold into batter.

2 Dip vegetables and turkey into batter. Fry in hot oil, a few at a time, until golden. Drain on kitchen paper. Serve with barbecue sauce.

300 Calories per portion

Prawn Toasties
SERVES 2

Wholemeal bread - *2 thick slices*
Peeled prawns - *100g (4oz)*
Cottage cheese - *100g (4oz)*
Garlic clove - *1, crushed*
Cheshire cheese - *50g (2oz) grated*
Sesame seeds - *5ml (1 tsp)*

METHOD
1 Toast one side of the bread.

2 Mix prawns, cottage cheese, garlic and half grated cheese. Spread onto untoasted side of the bread.

3 Sprinkle with remaining cheese and sesame seeds. Grill until heated through.

Tuna Cheese Paté
EACH RECIPE MAKES 4 ROUNDS

Tuna in brine - *198g can, drained*
Double Gloucester cheese - *100g (4oz) grated*

Lemon juice - *10ml (2 tsp)*
Low fat natural yogurt - *150g (5oz)*
Fresh parsley - *30ml (2 tbsp) chopped*

METHOD
1 Mash tuna, cheese and lemon juice. Blend in yogurt and parsley. Chill until firm. Serve as a sandwich filling, on toast or in a baked potato.

Cheesy Egg Spread

Eggs - *3 (size 3) hard boiled*
Low fat Cottage cheese - *225g (8oz)*
Reduced calorie salad cream - *45ml (3 tbsp)*
Red Leicester cheese - *25g (1 oz) grated*
Mustard and cress - *to garnish*

METHOD
1 Chop eggs and mash with cottage cheese and salad cream. Stir in grated cheese. Serve as a sandwich filling, on toast or in a baked potato.

345 Calories per portion

Lunch Box Rolls SERVES 4

Crusty rolls - *4*
Tuna in brine - *99g can, drained*
Low fat soft cheese - *225g (8oz)*
Red pepper - *25g (1 oz) de-seeded and diced*
Black pepper *freshly ground*
Red Leicester cheese - *75g (3oz) grated*
Creamed horseradish - *10ml (2 tsp)*

METHOD
1 Cut top off each roll and scoop out the centres.
2 Mix tuna, half the soft cheese and red pepper. Season.
3 Blend Red Leicester, remaining soft cheese and horseradish.
4. Use each filling to fill two rolls, pushing well in. Replace tops, wrap in foil and chill. Either serve whole or cut into 2.5cm (1 inch) slices.

385 Calories per portion

Mushroom Cups SERVES 4

Crusty rolls - *4*
Butter - *40g (1½ oz)*
Wholemeal flour - *25g (1 oz)*
Fresh milk - *300ml (½ pint)*
Button mushrooms - *50g (2oz) sliced*
Streaky bacon - *100g (4oz) well grilled and chopped*
Black pepper *freshly ground*
Fresh parsley - *15ml (1 tbsp) chopped*

METHOD
1 Cut top off each roll and scoop out the centres. Brush insides and tops with 25g (1 oz) melted butter and bake at 200°C (400°F), mark 6 until crisp.
2 Place flour, remaining butter and milk in a saucepan. Heat, stirring, until the sauce boils.
3 Add mushrooms. Cook for 2 minutes.
4 Stir in bacon, parsley and pepper.
5 Fill rolls, top with lids and serve immediately.

230 Calories per portion Ⓕ

Fish Cakes SERVES 4

Cooked haddock - *275g (10oz), skinned and boned*
Fresh milk - *225ml (8fl oz)*
Fresh parsley - *15ml (1 tbsp) chopped*
Onion - *1 medium, chopped*
Butter - *15g (½ oz)*
Potatoes - *350g (12oz) boiled*
Salt *and freshly ground* **black pepper**
Egg - *1 (size 3) beaten*
Wholemeal breadcrumbs - *to coat*

METHOD

1 Purée fish, milk and parsley in a processor or blender.

2 Gently fry onion in half the butter.

3 Mash potato with remaining butter and blend in the fish mixture and onions. Season.

4 Shape into 4 large or 8 small fish cakes, brush with egg and coat in breadcrumbs.

5 Grill under a medium heat for 5-10 minutes on each side or until cooked through and golden.

310 Calories per portion

Tuna Wedges SERVES 4

Tuna in brine - *250g (9oz) can, drained*
Natural yogurt - *150g (5oz)*
Dried mixed herbs - *5ml (1 tsp)*
Cornflour - *5ml (1 tsp)*
Self-raising flour - *75g (3oz)*
Wholemeal flour - *75g (3oz)*

Baking powder - *2.5ml (½ tsp)*
Salt *and freshly ground* **black pepper**
Butter - *50g (2oz)*
Fresh milk - *150ml (¼ pint)*

METHOD

1 Flake tuna. Mix with yogurt, herbs and cornflour.

2 Sift flours, baking powder and a pinch of salt into a bowl. Rub in butter and stir in approximately 100ml (4fl oz) milk to form a soft dough. Divide in two and roll each into 15cm (6 inch) rounds.

3 Place one round in the base of a 15cm (6 inch) deep cake tin, cover with filling and top with remaining round. Brush top with a little milk, score into 12 wedges and bake at 220°C (425°F), mark 7 for 25-30 minutes until golden.

335 Calories per portion

Fish & Soured Cream Bake   SERVES 4

White fish fillets - *450g (1 lb)*
Seasoned plain flour - *25g (1 oz)*
Fresh soured cream - *150g (5oz)*
Reduced calorie mayonnaise - *150g (5oz)*
Spring onions - *2, finely chopped*
Dried dill - *5ml (1 tsp)*
Lemon juice - *5ml (1 tsp)*
Applewood cheese - *50g (2oz) grated*
Fresh dill - *to garnish*

METHOD

1 Coat fish in seasoned flour. Place in a greased ovenproof dish.

2 Mix soured cream, mayonnaise, spring onions, dill and lemon juice and spoon over fish. Sprinkle with cheese.

3 Bake at 180°C (350°F), mark 4 for 30-35 minutes until fish flakes with a fork. Serve garnished with dill.

180 Calories per portion 🇫

Sole with Dill Sauce   SERVES 4

Lemon - *1 + slices to garnish*
Cooked rice - *50g (2oz)*
Green and red pepper - *50g (2oz) each, diced*
Mushrooms - *50g (2oz) sliced*
Sweetcorn - *50g (2oz)*
Fresh single cream - *75ml (5 tbsp)*

Salt *and freshly ground* black pepper
Fillets of sole - *4×100g (4oz), skinned*
Fresh milk - *200ml (7fl oz) approx.*
Butter - *25g (1 oz)*
Plain flour - *40g (1½ oz)*
Fresh dill - *10ml (2 tsp) chopped*

MICROWAVE INSTRUCTIONS

Grate lemon. Remove pith and dice flesh. Mix with rice, peppers, mushrooms, sweetcorn and cream.

Lay fillets on a board, skinned side up. Place filling in the centre. Season. Roll up, securing with a cocktail stick. Place in a dish, cover and cook on HIGH for 10-12 minutes. Drain off excess liquid. Make up to 300ml (½ pint) with milk.

Place butter in a bowl. Melt on HIGH for 30 seconds. Add flour and stir in the milk. Cook on HIGH for 3-4 minutes, stirring after each minute. Season and add dill. Pour over fish and garnish with slices of lemon.

Timings are for a 600 watt oven.

Fish

360 Calories per portion

Chopstick Fish with Noodles

SERVES 4

Noodles - *100g (4oz)*
Butter - *25g (1 oz)*
Soy sauce - *15ml (1 tbsp)*
Onion - *1 medium, finely chopped*
Celery - *3 sticks, finely chopped*
Mushrooms - *100g (4oz) chopped*
Plain flour - *25g (1 oz)*
Fresh milk - *450ml (¾ pint)*
Salt *and freshly ground* **black pepper**

Peanuts - *15ml (1 tbsp)*
Lemon - *½, grated rind only*
White fish - *450g (1 lb)*
skinned and cubed

METHOD

1 Cook noodles as directed on the packet. Drain. Toss in one third of the butter and soy sauce. Keep warm.

2 Melt remaining butter in a saucepan. Add onion, celery and mushrooms and cook gently for 5 minutes. Stir in flour, cook for 1 minute then gradually stir in milk. Bring to boil and cook for 2 minutes. Season.

3 Fold in nuts, lemon rind and fish and cook without stirring for 5 minutes. Serve with noodles.

NB: Omit peanuts if serving to young children.

390 Calories per portion

Kipper Soufflé

SERVES 4

Kippers - *3*
Cornflour - *25g (1 oz)*
Fresh milk - *450ml (¾ pint)*
Black pepper - *freshly ground*
Fresh parsley - *30ml (2 tbsp) chopped*
Eggs - *2 (size 3) separated*

METHOD

1 Stand kippers in a jug. Pour over boiling water to cover. Leave 5 minutes. Skin, bone and mash fillets with a fork.

2 Blend cornflour with 30ml (2 tbsp) milk. Pour into a saucepan with remaining milk and bring to the boil, stirring continuously. Cook for 1 minute. Add pepper, parsley and kippers. Remove pan from heat and beat in yolks. Cool.

3 Whisk whites until stiff, fold into kipper mixture and pour into a greased 568ml (1 pint) soufflé dish. Bake immediately at 200°C (400°F), mark 6 for 20 minutes. Serve at once.

Fish

55 Calories per portion Ⓕ

Mariner Pie

SERVES 6

Fresh mussels - *1kg (2.2 lb)*
Butter - *25g (1 oz)*
Lean pork - *225g (8oz) diced*
Onions - *2, finely chopped*
Carrots - *4, diced*
Pepper - *freshly ground*
Potatoes - *4 small, diced*

Fresh milk - *450ml (¾ pint)*
Bay leaves - *2*
Frozen puff pastry - *½ × 350g (12oz) thawed*

METHOD

Clean mussels and steam in a little water until the shells open. Discard any that do not open.

Melt butter in a saucepan. Add pork. Sauté for 5 minutes. Add onions and carrots and cook for 5 minutes. Add potato, milk and bay leaves. Season, bring to the boil and simmer for 15 minutes. Add mussels and pour into an ovenproof pie dish.

Roll out pastry and cover the pie. Brush with a little milk. Bake at 200°C (400°F), mark 6 for 25 minutes until puffed and golden.

55 Calories per portion Ⓕ

Smoked Haddock & Spinach Lasagne

SERVES 4

Smoked haddock - *450g (1 lb)*
Fresh milk - *450ml (¾ pint)*
Wholemeal flour - *30ml (2 tbsp)*
Butter - *25g (1 oz)*
English Cheddar cheese - *75g (3oz) grated*
Black pepper *freshly ground*
Spinach - *175g (6oz) cooked and well drained*
Wholemeal lasagne - *175g (6oz)*

METHOD

Skin haddock and poach in milk for 4-5 minutes. Drain, reserving the milk. Remove bones and flake fish.

Place flour, butter and reserved milk in a saucepan. Heat, stirring until the sauce boils. Cook for 2 minutes. Remove pan from the heat, stir in most of the cheese. Season.

Layer the spinach, lasagne, fish and sauce in a deep ovenproof dish, finishing with the sauce. Sprinkle with the remaining cheese and bake at 200°C (400°F), mark 6 for 30-35 minutes until golden.

25

305 Calories per portion Ⓕ

Gingered Monkfish Kebabs
SERVES 2

Butter - *15g (½ oz)*
Onion - *1 medium, sliced*
Fresh root ginger - *1cm (½ inch), peeled and chopped*
Garlic - *1 clove, crushed*
Red pepper - *½ chopped*
Cauliflower florets - *175g (6oz)*
Boned monkfish - *225g (8oz) cubed*
Turmeric - *large pinch*

Fresh milk - *150ml (¼ pint)*
Low fat soft cheese - *100g (4 oz)*
Chopped chives - *for garnish*

METHOD

1 Melt butter in a saucepan. Gently cook onion, ginger and garlic until soft.

2 Add pepper, cauliflower, fish and turmeric and cook for 2 minutes. Add milk, bring to the boil, cover and simmer for 5 minutes.

3 Blend soft cheese with a little of the hot sauce. Return to pan and heat gently through. Do not boil. Serve sprinkled with chives.

230 Calories per portion

Fish Kebabs
SERVES 4

Haddock fillets - *225g (8oz) skinned and cubed*
Button mushrooms - *8*
Tomatoes - *2, quartered*
Pineapple cubes in natural juice - *198g can, drained*
Butter - *50g (2oz)*
Plain flour - *25g (1 oz)*
Fresh milk - *300ml (½ pint)*
Tomato purée - *15ml (1 tbsp)*
Chilli powder - *2.5ml (½ tsp)*

METHOD

1 Thread fish, mushrooms, tomatoes and pineapple onto 4 skewers.

2 Melt 25g (1 oz) butter, brush over kebabs and grill, turning regularly, for 15 minutes.

3 Place flour, remaining butter and milk in a saucepan. Heat, stirring until the sauce boils. Blend in tomato purée and chilli powder and cook for 2 minutes. Serve with the kebabs.

Fish

Trout Soufflé Pancakes SERVES 6

Trout - *450g (1 lb), cleaned weight*
Fresh milk - *350ml (12fl oz)*
Butter - *25g (1 oz)*
Wholemeal flour - *75g (3oz)*

Creamed horseradish - *5ml (1 tsp)*
Black pepper *freshly ground*
Watercress - *1 bunch, trimmed and chopped*
Eggs - *3 (size 3) separated*

METHOD

1. Poach trout in 200ml (7fl oz) milk for 5 minutes. Reserve milk. Skin and flake the fish.

2. Place reserved milk, butter and 25g (1 oz) flour in a saucepan. Heat, stirring until the sauce boils. Cook for 2 minutes. Add horseradish and pepper.

3. Blanch watercress in boiling water. Drain well. Add with trout to the sauce. Stir in 2 egg yolks, cool slightly then fold in 2 stiffly beaten whites.

4. Sift remaining flour into a bowl. Beat in remaining egg and milk to give a smooth batter. Season. Use to make 6×15cm (6 inch) pancakes, as on page 66.

5. Cover each pancake with a layer of sauce and fold in half. Place on a greased baking sheet. Bake at 200°C (400°F), mark 6 for 20 minutes. Serve immediately.

Tropical Prawn Salad SERVES 4

Rice - *175g (6oz)*
Eating apples - *2, cored*
Banana - *1*
Lemon - *½, juice only*
Low fat soft cheese - *225g (8 oz)*
Curry powder - *15ml (1 tbsp)*
Fresh milk - *90ml (6 tbsp)*
Peeled prawns - *450g (1 lb)*
Green pepper - *1, diced*
Pineapple cubes in natural juice - *198g can, drained*
Chopped parsley - *for garnish*

METHOD

1. Cook rice as directed on the packet.

2. Cube apples. Slice banana. Dip both in lemon juice immediately and keep on separate plates.

3. Blend soft cheese, curry powder, remaining lemon juice and milk. Fold in the prawns and half the apples.

4. Stir banana, pepper, pineapple and remaining apples into the rice. Place on a serving dish, spoon over prawns and sprinkle with parsley.

310 Calories per portion

Trout with Watercress Sauce Serves 2

Watercress - *1 small bunch*
Lemon juice - *15ml (1 tbsp)*
Fillets of trout - *2×100g (4oz)*
Dry white wine - *45ml (3 tbsp)*
Made mustard - *2.5ml (½ tsp)*
Fresh soured cream - *150g (5oz)*

MICROWAVE INSTRUCTIONS

1 Reserve a few sprigs of watercress for garnish.
Place remainder in a bowl with lemon juice and 15ml
(1 tbsp) water. Cover and cook on HIGH for 1½ minutes.

2 Place fish in the base of a shallow dish. Pour over the
wine. Cover and cook on HIGH for 2½ minutes. Leave
to stand. Reserve liquor.

3 Purée watercress, mustard and cream in a processor
or liquidiser. Add fish liquor, pour into a jug and cook on
HIGH for 1 minute. Serve with fish and garnish with
watercress.

Timings are for a 600 watt oven.

---

545 Calories per portion

Salmon Leaves Serves 4

Fresh salmon - *450g (1 lb)*
Dry white wine - *150ml (¼ pint)*
Butter - *40g (1½ oz)*
Onion - *1 small, finely chopped*
Plain flour - *25g (1 oz)*
Fresh milk - *450ml (¾ pint)*

Lemon - *1, grated rind only*
Bayleaf - *1*
Fresh tarragon - *7.5ml (1½ tsp)*
Fresh soured cream - *75g (3oz)*
Filo pastry - *6-8 sheets*

METHOD

1 Gently poach salmon in wine for 5 minutes. Drain and reserve the juices.
Skin, bone and flake the fish.

2 Melt 15g (½ oz) butter in a saucepan and gently cook onion until soft.
Add flour and milk. Heat, stirring continuously until the
sauce boils. Add rind, bayleaf and tarragon and simmer
for 5 minutes. Remove bayleaf. Fold soured cream,
fish and reserved juice into the sauce.

3 Melt remaining butter. Lightly brush over base
and sides of a square tin. Line tin with filo pastry and
brush lightly with butter. Layer the salmon mixture
and remaining filo in the tin, finishing with filo.
Brush with butter. Bake at 190°C (375°F),
mark 5 for 20-35 minutes until golden.

370 Calories per portion Ⓕ

Salmon with Fennel SERVES 4

Fennel - *1 medium head, chopped*
Butter - *15g (½ oz)*
Salmon steaks - *4×150g (5oz)*
Lemon juice - *30ml (2 tbsp)*
Salt *and freshly ground* **black pepper**
Plain flour - *15g (½ oz)*
Fresh milk - *300ml (½ pint)*
Lemon and fennel leaves - *for garnish*

METHOD
1 Cook fennel in salted water for 10 minutes until soft. Drain.

2 Melt butter in a frying pan. Add salmon, lemon juice and seasoning. Cook gently, turning once, for 10 minutes. Remove salmon from the pan.

3 Add flour and milk to the pan. Heat, stirring continuously, until the sauce boils. Cook for 2 minutes. Add the fennel. Purée in a food processor or blender until smooth. Reheat gently. Serve with the salmon and garnish with lemon and fennel leaves.

375 Calories per portion

Haddock in Lemon Butter Sauce SERVES 4

Haddock fillets - *450g (1 lb) skinned*
Fresh milk - *300ml (½ pint)*
Lemon - *1, grated rind only*
Salt *and freshly ground* **black pepper**
Cornflour - *15ml (1 tbsp)* + *30ml (2 tbsp) milk*
Butter - *20g (¾ oz)*
Fresh parsley - *for garnish*

METHOD
1 Cut haddock into 4 portions. Place in a frying pan with milk, lemon rind and seasoning. Simmer gently for 8 minutes. Gently remove fish and keep warm.

2 Blend cornflour and milk. Add to poaching liquid. Bring to the boil, stirring continuously and cook for 2 minutes. Add butter. Spoon sauce over the fish and garnish with parsley.

350 Calories per portion

Chicken Salad SERVES 4

Cooked chicken - *350g (12oz)*
Cooked brown rice - *100g (4oz)*
Blue Cheshire cheese - *100g (4oz) cubed*
Eating apples - *2, cored and diced*
Radishes - *50g (2oz) sliced*
Celery - *2 sticks, sliced*
Sultanas - *25g (1 oz)*
Low fat natural yogurt - *150g (5oz)*
Mayonnaise - *15ml (1 tbsp)*
Red skinned apple - *for garnish*

METHOD

1 Combine chicken, rice, cheese, apples, radishes, celery and sultanas.

2 Blend the yogurt and mayonnaise and fold through the chicken mixture. Chill. Serve garnished with apple slices.

325 Calories per portion **F**

Chicken and Asparagus Pie SERVES 6

Butter - *25g (1 oz)*
Carrots - *2, sliced*
Button onions - *8*
Button mushrooms - *100g (4oz) halved*
Wholemeal flour - *20g (³/₄ oz)*
Fresh milk - *450ml (³/₄ pint)*
Cooked chicken - *350g (12oz), cut in strips*
Canned asparagus - *1 small can, drained*

Salt *and freshly ground* **black pepper**
Fresh single cream - *30ml (2 tbsp)*
Flaky pastry - *¹/₂×350g (12oz) packet*

METHOD

1 Melt butter in a saucepan and gently cook carrots, onions and mushrooms for 5 minutes. Stir in flour, gradually add milk and bring to the boil, stirring continuously. Cook for 2 minutes.

2 Add chicken, asparagus, seasoning and cream to the sauce. Pour into a 1.1 litre (2 pint) pie dish.

3 Roll pastry to fit top of the dish, dampen the rim and cover. Brush with milk. Bake at 200°C (400°F), mark 6 for 25 minutes until golden.

500 Calories per portion Ⓕ

Chicken Pimento SERVES 4

Boneless chicken breasts - *4×150g (5oz)*
Butter - *15g (½ oz)*
Garlic - *1 clove, crushed*
Pimentos - *200g can, well drained and sliced*
English Cheddar cheese - *100g (4oz) grated*
Fresh double cream - *150ml (¼ pint)*
Fresh milk - *150ml (¼ pint)*
Red pepper - *for garnish*

METHOD

1 Remove skin from chicken breasts. Melt butter in a frying pan. Gently cook chicken and garlic for 15-20 minutes until thoroughly cooked. Keep warm.

2 Blend pimentos, cheese and cream in a food processor or blender with a little of the milk. Transfer to a saucepan, add remaining milk and heat gently, stirring, until cheese melts. Pour over chicken and serve garnished with pepper.

---

220 Calories per portion

Tandoori Chicken SERVES 4

Garlic - *2-3 cloves, crushed*
Low fat natural yogurt - *300g (10oz)*
Garam masala - *10ml (2 tsp)*
Paprika - *5ml (1 tsp)*
Ground ginger - *5ml (1 tsp)*
Chilli powder - *2.5ml (½ tsp)*
Dry mustard - *2.5ml (½ tsp)*
Turmeric - *2.5ml (½ tsp)*
Boneless chicken breasts - *4×150g (5oz)*

METHOD

1 Blend garlic, yogurt and spices in a large bowl.

2 Remove skin and cut a few slashes into the flesh of the chicken. Place in the yogurt mixture, cover and leave in the refrigerator overnight.

3 Drain chicken, place on a roasting rack and bake at 200°C (400°F), mark 6 for 40 minutes until cooked through and brown.

This could also be cooked on a barbecue but be sure to cook it thoroughly.

255 Calories per portion

Chicken Chaudfroid SERVES 4

Chicken joints - *4, skinned*
Bouquet garni - *1*
Aspic crystals - *25g (1 oz)*
Plain flour - *25g (1 oz)*
Butter - *15g (½ oz)*
Fresh milk - *450ml (¾ pint)*
Gelatine - *11g sachet*
Mushrooms, pimento and parsley - *for garnish*

METHOD

1 Poach chicken in water with bouquet garni until thoroughly cooked. Allow to cool in the liquid. Make up aspic as directed on the packet, using poaching liquid.

2 Place flour, butter and milk in a saucepan. Heat, stirring, until the sauce boils. Cook for 2 minutes. Cool.

3 Sprinkle gelatine over 45ml (3 tbsp) warm aspic. Heat until dissolved then stir into sauce.

4 Place chicken on a wire rack. Coat twice with sauce, allowing it to set between coats. Garnish then baste with cold liquid aspic. Allow to set before touching.

---

350 Calories per portion 🅕

Cheshire Chicken SERVES 4

Chicken breast fillets - *4×125g (4oz) skinned*
Spinach leaves - *8 large, trimmed*
Blue Cheshire cheese - *100g (4oz)*
Plain flour - *25g (1 oz)*
Egg - *1 (size 3) beaten*
Wholemeal breadcrumbs - *100g (4oz) toasted*

METHOD

1 Place chicken fillets between 2 sheets greaseproof paper and flatten with a rolling pin.

2 Blanch spinach in boiling water for a few seconds. Plunge in cold water, drain and dry on kitchen paper.

3 Cut cheese into 4 fingers and wrap in spinach leaves. Place in the centre of each fillet and fold up like an envelope, securing with wooden cocktail sticks. Chill for 15 minutes.

4 Coat chicken in flour, then egg, then breadcrumbs. Place on a greased baking sheet. Bake at 200°C (400°F), mark 6 for 40 minutes until golden.

400 Calories per portion Ⓕ

Suprêmes Gratinées SERVES 4

Spinach - *50g (2oz) cooked and chopped*
Wholemeal breadcrumbs - *25g (1 oz)*
Garlic - *1 clove, crushed*
Lemon - *½, grated rind only*
Red Leicester cheese - *100g (4oz) grated*
Fresh milk - *450ml (¾ pint)*
Chicken suprêmes - *4×125g (4oz)*
Butter - *25g (1 oz)*
Wholemeal flour - *25g (1 oz)*
Black pepper *freshly ground*

METHOD

1 Mix spinach, breadcrumbs, garlic, lemon rind and half cheese with 30ml (2 tbsp) milk. Shape stuffing into 4 ovals. Place one in the pocket of each suprême.

2 Melt half butter and lightly fry the suprêmes. Place in an ovenproof dish.

3 Place remaining butter, flour and milk in a saucepan. Heat stirring until the sauce boils. Cook for 2 minutes. Remove from heat, add remaining cheese and stir until melted. Season. Pour over chicken and bake at 190°C (375°F), mark 5 for 30 minutes.

275 Calories per portion

Fruity Chicken SERVES 4

Chicken meat - *350g (12oz) cubed*
Seasoned flour - *15-30ml (1-2 tbsp)*
Butter - *25g (1 oz)*
Onion - *1 small, chopped*
Chilli powder - *5ml (1 tsp)*
Fresh milk - *300ml (½ pint)*
Tomato purée - *15ml (1 tbsp)*
Ground ginger - *2.5ml (½ tsp)*
Banana - *1×175g (6oz) sliced*
Pineapple pieces - *213g can, drained*

METHOD

1 Coat chicken in seasoned flour. Melt butter in a large saucepan, add chicken, onion, chilli powder and cook gently for 5 minutes.

2 Gradually add milk and heat, stirring, until the sauce boils. Cook for 2 minutes. Add tomato purée and ginger. Cover and simmer for 30 minutes until chicken is cooked, adding banana and pineapple for the final 5 minutes. Serve with rice.

410 Calories per portion

Turkey & Cranberry Gougère SERVES 4

Butter - *65g (2½ oz)*
Onion - *1 small, chopped*
Fresh cranberries - *75g (3oz)*
Plain flour - *65g (2½ oz)*
Fresh milk - *325ml (11fl oz)*
Orange - *1, zest and juice*

Cooked turkey - *350g (12oz) cubed*
Eggs - *2 (size 3), beaten*

METHOD

1 Melt 15g (½ oz) butter in a saucepan and gently cook onion and cranberries. Stir in 15g (½ oz) flour and cook for 1 minute.

2 Gradually add 175ml (6fl oz) milk and heat, stirring until the sauce boils. Cook for 2 minutes. Add orange zest and juice and turkey. Spoon into a 900ml (1½ pint) ovenproof dish.

3 Heat 150ml (¼ pint) milk and 50g (2oz) butter in a saucepan. Beat in 50g (2oz) sifted flour. Cool slightly then beat in eggs. Transfer to a piping bag and pipe around the edge of the dish. Bake at 200°C (400°F), mark 6 for 35-40 minutes.

---

345 Calories per portion Ⓕ

Turkey à la Crème SERVES 4

Butter - *7g (⅓ oz)*
Onion - *50g (2oz) sliced*
Cooked turkey - *350g (12oz) cut in strips*
Red pepper - *1, de-seeded and sliced*
Dry white wine - *150ml (¼ pint)*
Salt *and freshly ground* **black pepper**
Fresh double cream - *150ml (¼ pint)*
Sweetcorn - *100g (4oz)*

METHOD

1 Melt butter in a saucepan. Add onion, turkey, red pepper, wine and seasoning. Bring to the boil and simmer for 15 minutes.

2 Stir in cream and sweetcorn, reheat gently and serve with rice.

365 Calories per portion Ⓕ

Turkey & Broccoli Supper SERVES 4

Broccoli florets - *175g (6oz)*
Plain flour - *25g (1 oz)*
Butter - *15g (½ oz)*
Fresh milk - *300ml (½ pint)*
Salt *and freshly ground* **black pepper**
English Cheddar cheese - *100g (4oz) grated*
Flaked almonds - *50g (2oz) toasted*
Garlic - *1 clove, crushed*
Cooked turkey - *225g (8oz) cubed*

METHOD

1 Blanch broccoli in boiling salted water for 3 minutes.
Drain.

2 Place flour, butter and milk in a saucepan. Heat, stirring,
until the sauce boils. Cook for 2 minutes. Season.
Remove pan from heat.

3 Add 75g (3oz) cheese, 40g (1½ oz) almonds, garlic, turkey
and broccoli. Transfer to an overproof dish and sprinkle
with remaining cheese and almonds. Bake at 190°C (375°F),
mark 5 for 15-20 minutes.

240 Calories per portion

Spicy Turkey Kebabs SERVES 4

Turkey meat - *450g (1 lb) cubed*
Peanut butter - *60ml (4 tbsp)*
Ground cumin - *5ml (1 tsp)*
Chilli powder - *5ml (1 tsp)*
Fresh milk - *150ml (¼ pint)*
Creamy fromage frais - *175g (6oz)*
Lime wedges - *to serve*

METHOD

1 Thread turkey onto skewers and arrange in a shallow dish.

2 Blend peanut butter, spices and milk. Pour over kebabs
and refrigerate for at least 2 hours, turning several times.

3 Grill kebabs until cooked, turning frequently.

4 Place remaining marinade in a saucepan and bring to the
boil. Simmer for 5 minutes. Remove from heat,
stir in fromage frais and reheat without boiling.
Serve kebabs with sauce and wedges of lime.

Beef

330 Calories per portion

Pasticcio — SERVES 6

Lean minced beef - *225g (8oz)*
Lean bacon - *50g (2oz) chopped*
Onion - *50g (2oz) chopped*
Carrot - *50g (2oz) chopped*
Celery - *1 stick, sliced*
Garlic - *1 clove, crushed*
Tomato purée - *30ml (2 tbsp)*
Beef stock - *225ml (8fl oz)*

Cooked macaroni - *225g (8oz)*
Frozen peas - *175g (6oz)*
Butter - *25g (1 oz)*
Plain flour - *50g (2oz)*
Fresh milk - *568ml (1 pint)*
Double Gloucester cheese - *50g (2oz) grated*
Salt *and freshly ground* **black pepper**

METHOD
1 Dry fry mince, bacon and onion.
Drain off excess fat. Add carrot, celery, garlic,
tomato purée and stock. Simmer for 1 hour.
Add macaroni and peas. Place in an ovenproof dish.

2 Place butter, flour and milk in a saucepan. Heat,
stirring, until the sauce boils. Cook for 2 minutes.
Remove from heat and stir in half cheese. Season and
pour over beef. Sprinkle with remaining cheese.
Bake at 180°C (350°F), mark 4 for 30 minutes.

495 Calories per portion **F**

Calzone Bolognese — SERVES 4

Dried yeast - *15g (½ oz)*
Sugar - *large pinch*
Salt - *2.5ml (½ tsp)*
Strong plain flour - *350g (12oz)*
Butter - *40g (1½ oz)*
Fresh milk - *225ml (8fl oz) warmed*

Lean minced beef - *350g (12oz)*
Onion - *75g (3oz) chopped*
Red pepper - *1, seeded and chopped*
Garlic - *2 cloves, crushed*
Fresh mixed herbs - *5ml (1 tsp)*

Chopped tomatoes - *397g can*
Tomato purée - *15ml (1 tbsp)*
Worcestershire sauce - *15ml (1 tbs*
Black pepper *freshly ground*
Mozzarella - *100g (4oz) grated*

METHOD
1 Mix yeast, sugar, salt and flour. Rub in butter. Mix to a soft dough with milk.
Knead and leave to prove for 1-1½ hours until doubled in size.

2 Dry fry mince, onion, pepper, garlic and herbs for
10 minutes. Add tomatoes, purée, Worcestershire
sauce and season. Cook for 5 minutes.

3 Knead dough, cut into 4, knead again and roll out
4 × 15cm (6 inch) circles. Cover half each circle with
sauce, sprinkle with Mozzarella cheese, moisten
rim with milk, fold in half and seal. Brush with
milk and bake at 200°C (400°F), mark 6 for
20 minutes until golden.

315 Calories per portion (F)

Chilli Cobbler SERVES 4

Lean minced beef - *225g (8oz)*
Onion - *100g (4oz) chopped*
Chilli powder - *5ml (1 tsp)*
Tomatoes - *213g can*
Red kidney beans - *213g can, drained*
Wholemeal flour - *100g (4oz)*
Baking powder - *5ml (1 tsp)*
Butter - *25g (1 oz)*
Fresh milk - *150ml (¼ pint)*

METHOD

1 Dry fry mince, onion and chilli powder in a large saucepan.
Add tomatoes and kidney beans and simmer for 10 minutes.

2 Sift flour and baking powder. Rub in butter and stir in most of
the milk to give a soft dough. Roll to 1cm (½ inch) thick and cut out
5cm (2 inch) circles.

3 Transfer mince to a 568ml (1 pint) ovenproof dish. Arrange
scones, overlapping, around the edge. Brush with milk.
Bake at 200°C (400°F), mark 6 for 10 minutes until
scones have risen and are brown.

365 Calories per portion

Cabbage Parcels SERVES 4

Cabbage leaves - *12*
Brown rice - *75g (3oz)*
Lean minced beef - *225g (8oz)*
Onion - *50g (2oz) chopped*
Dried oregano - *5ml (1 tsp)*
Tomato purée - *30ml (2 tbsp)*
Beef stock - *225ml (8fl oz)*
Butter - *15g (½ oz)*
Plain flour - *25g (1 oz)*

Fresh milk - *450ml (¾ pint)*
Allspice - *2.5ml (½ tsp)*
Red Leicester - *100g (4oz) grated*

METHOD

1 Cook cabbage in boiling salted water until tender.
Cook rice according to packet instructions. Drain.

2 Dry fry mince and onion until brown. Drain off fat.

3 Mix oregano, tomato purée and stock. Boil until
reduced by half. Stir in rice and mince mixture.
Keep warm.

4 Place butter, flour and milk in a saucepan. Heat,
stirring, until the sauce boils. Cook for 2 minutes.
Remove from heat, stir in allspice and cheese.

5 Place a spoonful of filling on each cabbage leaf.
Fold in the sides to make a parcel. Serve with
sauce and any remaining filling.

475 Calories per portion **F**

Beef Olives SERVES 4

Minced beef or pork - *225g (8oz)*
Streaky bacon - *50g (2oz) minced*
Wholemeal breadcrumbs - *25g (1 oz)*
Allspice - *5ml (1 tsp)*
Salt *and freshly ground* **black pepper**
Fresh parsley - *30ml (2 tbsp)*
Egg - *1 (size 3) beaten*

Braising steak - *4 thin slices*
Butter - *25g (1 oz)*
Button onions - *12*
Garlic - *1 clove, crushed*
Wholemeal flour - *25g (1 oz)*
Beef stock cube - *1*
Fresh milk - *450ml (¾ pint) warmed*

METHOD

1 Combine mince, bacon, breadcrumbs, allspice, seasoning, parsley and egg. Beat out steak slices, place stuffing on each slice and roll up. Tie with string to secure.

2 Melt butter in a frying pan. Cook onions and garlic for 2 minutes. Add beef, brown all over then cook for 10 minutes. Remove beef from the pan and keep warm.

3 Stir flour into onions and juices. Gradually add milk, sprinkle in stock cube and bring to boil, stirring continuously. Add beef and simmer for 35 minutes until tender.

250 Calories per portion **F**

Corned Beef Hash Flan SERVES 6

Plain flour - *50g (2oz)*
Wholemeal flour - *50g (2oz)*
Butter - *65g (2½ oz)*
Salt *and freshly ground* **black pepper**
Fresh milk - *175ml (6fl oz)*
Onion - *50g (2oz)*
Green pepper - *1 small, de-seeded and chopped*
Potatoes - *175g (6oz) peeled and diced*

Fresh parsley - *30ml (2 tbsp) chopped*
Corned beef - *198g can, diced*

METHOD

1 Place flours in a bowl. Rub in 50g (2oz) butter until mixture resembles fine breadcrumbs. Season. Add 30ml (2 tbsp) milk and mix to a dough. Roll out and use to line a 18cm (7 inch) flan ring. Bake blind at 190°C (375°F), mark 5 for 15 minutes.

2 Melt remaining butter and cook onion, pepper and potatoes for 5 minutes. Add remaining milk and simmer for 10 minutes. Add parsley and corned beef. Season. Cook uncovered until all liquid is absorbed. Pile into the pastry case. Reheat in the oven for 10 minutes.

455 Calories per portion Ⓕ

Hungarian Goulash SERVES 6

Butter - *25g (1 oz)*
Onions - *2, chopped*
Garlic - *1 clove, crushed*
Carrots - *2, sliced*
Dried marjoram - *5ml (1 tsp)*
Paprika - *30ml (2 tbsp)*
Stewing steak - *450g (1 lb) cubed*

Seasoned wholemeal flour - *45ml (3 tbsp)*
Fresh milk - *900ml (1½ pint)*
Potatoes - *3, scrubbed and quartered*
Wholemeal self-raising flour - *100g (4 oz)*
Suet - *50g (2oz)*
Dried mixed herbs - *15ml (1 tbsp)*
Fresh soured cream - *45ml (3 tbsp)*

METHOD

1 Melt butter in a large saucepan and gently cook onions, garlic, carrots, marjoram and paprika for 5 minutes.

2 Toss steak in seasoned flour and add to pan. Gradually stir in milk, cover and simmer for 1 hour or until meat is tender. Add potatoes and simmer for 30 minutes.

3 Mix self-raising flour, suet, herbs, seasoning, soured cream and sufficient water to give a firm dough. Form into dumplings, drop into goulash, cover and simmer for 15 minutes until well risen.

330 Calories per portion

Spiced Beef Bake SERVES 4

Lean minced beef - *450g (1 lb)*
Onion - *75g (3oz) chopped*
Chilli seasoning mix - *15ml (1 tbsp)*
Ready-to-eat dried apricots - *40g (1½ oz)*
Eggs - *2 (size 3)*
Fresh milk - *300ml (½ pint)*
Flaked almonds - *for topping*

METHOD

1 Dry fry mince and drain off excess fat. Add onion and chilli seasoning and cook for 2 minutes. Chop then add apricots and pour into a shallow ovenproof dish.

2 Whisk eggs and milk, season lightly and pour over meat. Sprinkle with almonds and bake at 200°C (400°F), mark 6 for 40-45 minutes, until set.

405 Calories per portion

Lamb & Broccoli Parcels SERVES 4

Plain flour - *100g (4oz)*
Salt *and freshly ground* **black pepper**
Dried parsley - *10ml (2 tsp)*
Dried thyme - *2.5ml (½ tsp)*
Egg - *1 (size 3), beaten*
Fresh milk - *300ml (½ pint)*

Carrots - *2 medium, cut in fine strips*
Fresh broccoli - *2 heads broken into florets*
Noisettes of lamb - *4*
Red wine - *150ml (¼ pint)*
Redcurrant jelly - *15ml (1 tbsp)*
Melted butter - *to brush pancakes*
Lemon zest - *pared strips for decoration*

METHOD

1 Sift flour, seasoning and herbs into a basin. Beat in the egg, half the milk, then remaining milk to give a smooth batter. Use to make 4×20.5cm (8 inch) pancakes, as on page 66. Keep warm.

2 Blanch carrots and broccoli in boiling water for 2 minutes. Drain.

3 Grill lamb until cooked through, slice thinly and keep warm.

4 Transfer lamb juices to a saucepan. Add wine and redcurrant jelly. Boil rapidly until slightly syrupy.

5 Arrange lamb in the centre of each pancake. Sprinkle with vegetables then a little sauce. Fold to make parcels. Lightly brush with melted butter. Grill gently for 5 minutes. Garnish with lemon zest and serve with remaining sauce.

460 Calories per portion

Minted Lamb SERVES 4

Chump chops - *4×150g (5oz)*
Garlic - *2 cloves, crushed*
Crème de menthe - *45ml (3 tbsp)*
Fresh double cream - *150ml (¼ pint)*
Fresh milk - *75ml (5 tbsp)*
Fresh mint - *for garnish*

METHOD

1 Dry fry chops with garlic for 15 minutes or until brown and cooked through. Remove from the pan and keep warm.

2 Add crème de menthe, cream and milk to the pan. Heat gently but do not boil. Serve sauce with the chops and garnish with mint.

Lamb

360 Calories per portion Ⓕ

Arabian Lamb SERVES 4

Butter - *15g (½ oz)*
Onion - *75g (3oz) chopped*
Garlic - *1 clove, crushed*
Leg chops - *4 × 150g (5oz)*
Turmeric - *5ml (1 tsp)*
Ground cinnamon - *2.5ml (½ tsp)*
Ground ginger - *2.5ml (½ tsp)*
Bay leaves - *2*
Wholemeal flour - *15ml (1 tbsp)*
Fresh milk - *300ml (½ pint)*
Dried apricots - *12, soaked*

METHOD

1 Melt butter in a saucepan, add onion and garlic and cook until soft.

2 Add lamb, spices and bay leaves. Season and cook until brown. Stir in the flour, gradually add milk and bring to the boil. Simmer for 30 minutes or until lamb is tender, adding apricots for the final 5 minutes.

---

380 Calories per portion Ⓕ

Lamb Korma SERVES 4

Butter - *15g (½ oz)*
Onion - *75g (3oz)*
Garlic - *2 cloves, crushed*
Fresh ginger - *5cm (2 inch) peeled and grated*
Ground coriander - *10ml (2 tsp)*
Ground cumin - *10ml (2 tsp)*
Turmeric - *5ml (1 tsp)*
Ground cinnamon - *2.5ml (½ tsp)*

Lean leg or shoulder of lamb - *450g (1 lb), cubed*
Cashew nuts - *50g (2oz)*
Low fat natural yogurt - *300g (10oz)*
Fresh coriander - *30ml (2 tbsp)*
Fresh mint - *for garnish*

METHOD

1 Melt butter in a large saucepan. Gently cook onion and garlic until soft. Add grated ginger and spices and cook for a few minutes.

2 Add lamb, cashew nuts, half the yogurt and coriander. Simmer gently for 30 minutes or until tender. Serve with remaining yogurt and mint.

545 Calories per portion Ⓕ

Pork with Dumplings SERVES 4

Wholemeal flour - *200g (7oz)*
Fresh thyme - *7.5ml (1½ tsp)*
Paprika - *5ml (1 tsp)*
Lean pork - *450g (1 lb) diced*
Butter - *40g (1½ oz)*
Mushrooms - *150g (5oz) sliced*
Leeks - *2, sliced*

Fresh milk - *568ml (1 pint)*
Baking powder - *10ml (2 tsp)*
Poppy seeds - *10ml (2 tsp)*
Fresh chives - *10ml (2 tsp) chopped*
Egg - *1 (size 3) beaten*
Wholemeal breadcrumbs - *45ml (3 tbsp)*

METHOD

1 Mix 50g (2oz) flour, thyme and paprika. Use to coat the pork.

2 Melt butter in a saucepan. Add mushrooms, pork and leeks. Cook for 5 minutes. Add any remaining coating flour. Gradually blend in 450ml (¾ pint) milk, heat, stirring until sauce boils. Simmer 30 minutes, until pork is tender.

3 Mix remaining flour, baking powder, poppy seeds, chives, egg, breadcrumbs and milk to form a soft dough. Form into dumplings, place on top of the pork, cover and cook for 15 minutes until well risen.

---

375 Calories per portion

Curried Pork Pancakes SERVES 4

Plain flour - *115g (4½ oz)*
Salt - *large pinch*
Egg - *1 (size 3)*
Fresh milk - *450ml (¾ pint)*
Butter - *25g (1 oz) plus for cooking pancakes*

Curry powder - *5-10ml (1-2 tsp)*
Sultanas - *25g (1 oz)*
Cooked lean pork - *225g (8oz) cubed*
Cooking apple - *1, peeled, diced and cooked*

METHOD

1 Sift 100g (4oz) flour and salt into a bowl. Make a well, break in egg and beat with a wooden spoon. Slowly beat in 300ml (½ pint) milk to give a smooth batter.

2 Using a 18cm (7 inch) frying pan, use batter to make 6 pancakes, as on page 66.

3 Melt 25g (1 oz) butter in a saucepan. Add curry powder and cook for 1 minute. Add remaining flour and milk. Heat, stirring continuously, until sauce boils. Add sultanas, pork and apple. Cook for 2 minutes. Divide mixture between pancakes, roll up and serve.

Pork & Ham

Pork 'n' Tomato Parcels SERVES 4

Lean pork chops - *4 × 175g (6oz)*
Seasoned flour - *30ml (2 tbsp)*
Butter - *15g (½ oz)*
Onion - *75g (3oz) sliced*
Garlic - *1 clove, crushed*
Tomatoes - *350g (12oz) skinned*
Dried thyme - *5ml (1 tsp)*
Worcestershire sauce - *10ml (2 tsp)*
Fresh double cream - *150ml (¼ pint)*
Fresh parsley - *10ml (2 tsp) chopped*

METHOD

1 Coat chops in flour. Melt butter in a frying pan and brown chops on both sides. Place each on a large square of foil. Add onion and garlic to pan.

2 Chop the tomatoes. Add to the pan with the thyme and Worcestershire sauce. Cook for 5 minutes. Remove from heat. Add cream and parsley and divide between the 4 chops. Loosely wrap and bake at 190°C (375°F), mark 5 for 40 minutes until tender.

Pork Crumble SERVES 4

Lean pork - *450g (1 lb) diced*
Butter - *65g (2½ oz)*
Wholemeal flour - *150g (5oz)*
Fresh milk - *450ml (¾ pint)*
Salt *and freshly ground* **black pepper**
Fresh sage - *10ml (2 tsp) chopped*
Mushrooms - *100g (4oz) sliced*
Leeks - *4, sliced*

Mustard powder - *5ml (1 tsp)*
Paprika - *5ml (1 tsp)*
English Cheddar cheese - *50g (2oz) grated*
Porridge oats - *25g (1 oz)*

METHOD

1 Fry pork in 15g (½ oz) butter until brown. Add 25g (1 oz) flour and gradually stir in milk. Season. Heat, stirring, until sauce boils. Cover and simmer for 45 minutes. Add sage, mushrooms and leeks. Simmer for 10 minutes. Pour into a greased shallow ovenproof dish.

2 Rub remaining butter and flour together. Add mustard, paprika, cheese and oats. Sprinkle over the pork. Bake at 200°C (400°F), mark 6 for 25 minutes until golden.

600 Calories per portion

Pasta Supper

SERVES 4

Tagliatelle - *275g (10oz)*
Butter - *15g (½ oz)*
Onion - *150g (5oz)*
Frozen sweetcorn - *175g (6oz)*
Frozen peas - *175g (6oz)*
Stock - *150ml (¼ pint)*
Cornflour - *15ml (1 tbsp)*
Fresh single cream - *300ml (½ pint)*

Cooked smoked ham - *100g (4oz) cut in strips*
Caerphilly cheese - *50g (2oz) grated*
Black pepper *freshly ground*

METHOD

1 Cook pasta in boiling salted water as directed on packet.

2 Melt butter in a saucepan and cook onion until soft. Add sweetcorn, peas and stock. Cook for 4 minutes.

3 Blend cornflour with a little cold water, add to pan with the cream and ham. Heat gently until thickened. Stir into the pasta and serve sprinkled with cheese and black pepper.

350 Calories per portion

Tasty Courgette Bake

SERVES 4

Courgettes - *700g (1½ lb) sliced*
Smoked streaky bacon - *75g (3oz) rinded and chopped*
Onion - *150g (5oz) sliced*
Eggs - *3 (size 3)*

Fresh milk - *300ml (½ pint)*
Dried marjoram - *2.5ml (½ tsp)*
Salt *and freshly ground* **black pepper**
English Cheddar cheese - *100g (4oz) grated*

METHOD

1 Blanch courgettes in boiling water for 2 minutes. Drain and cool.

2 Dry fry bacon and onion in a non-stick pan for 2 minutes, stirring frequently.

3 Lightly grease an ovenproof dish. Arrange courgettes, bacon and onion in the base.

4 Beat eggs, milk, herbs, seasoning and 75g (3oz) cheese together. Pour over the courgettes. Sprinkle with remaining cheese. Bake at 180°C (350°F), mark 4 for 55 minutes until set and golden.

480 Calories per burger in a bap **Ⓕ**

Pork 'n' Cheese Burgers SERVES 4

Lean minced pork - *450g (1 lb)*
Taco seasoning mix - *15ml (1 tbsp)*
Lancashire cheese - *100g (4oz) grated*
Egg - *1 (size 3)*
Baps and salad - *to serve*

METHOD

1 Place pork in a bowl and break up with a fork. Add taco seasoning, most of the cheese and egg, beating well to combine.

2 Shape into 4 burgers — it is easier with wet hands. Grill or dry fry until browned and thoroughly cooked through. Sprinkle with remaining cheese and grill until melted. Serve in warm baps.

525 Calories per portion

Savoury Hedgehog SERVES 4

Potatoes - *900g (2lb) peeled*
Salt
Butter - *25g (1 oz)*

Fresh milk - *150ml (¼ pint)*
Egg - *1 (size 3)*
Chipolata sausages - *450g (1 lb)*

METHOD

1 Cook potatoes in boiling salted water until tender. Drain. Mash with butter, egg and milk. Arrange in a hedgehog shape on an ovenproof dish. Bake at 190°C (375°F), mark 5 for 10 minutes. Keep warm.

2 Grill sausages. Cut all but one in half. Arrange halved sausages like hedgehog spines. Cut remaining sausage to make eyes and snout. Serve hot with baked beans.

590 Calories per portion

Tagliatelle Supper SERVES 4

Butter - *20g (¾ oz)*
Button mushrooms - *175g (6oz) sliced*
Wholemeal flour - *40g (1½ oz)*
Fresh milk - *568ml (1 pint)*
Salt *and freshly ground* **black pepper**
Back bacon - *4 rashers*
English Cheddar cheese - *100g (4oz) grated*
Tagliatelle - *225g (8oz)*

METHOD

1 Melt butter in a saucepan. Gently cook mushrooms
until soft. Add flour and gradually add milk. Heat,
stirring, until sauce boils. Season.
Cook for 2 minutes.

2 Grill and chop bacon. Add to sauce.

3 Cook tagliatelle as directed on the packet.
Drain and stir in cheese. Serve with bacon sauce.

415 Calories per portion **F**

Stuffed Cheesy Courgettes SERVES 4

Courgettes - *4 medium, halved*
Streaky bacon - *4 rashers, chopped*
Onion - *175g (6oz) chopped*
Brown rice - *75g (3oz) cooked weight*
Tomatoes - *3 medium, skinned and chopped*
Sweetcorn - *200g can, drained*
Prepared English mustard - *5ml (1 tsp)*
Fresh parsley - *15ml (1 tbsp) chopped*
English Cheddar cheese - *100g (4oz)*
Fresh single cream - *60ml (4 tbsp)*

Salt *and freshly ground* **black pepper**
Butter - *25g (1 oz)*
Plain flour - *15g (½ oz)*
Fresh milk - *300ml (½ pint)*
Wholemeal breadcrumbs - *25g (1 oz)*

METHOD

1 Cook courgettes in boiling salted water for
10 minutes. Drain and scoop out flesh. Place
shells in a lightly greased ovenproof dish.

2 Dry fry bacon and onion in a saucepan until
golden. Add rice, tomatoes, sweetcorn, mustard,
parsley, half cheese and cream. Season and fill courgettes.

3 Place butter, flour and milk in a saucepan. Heat, stirring until
sauce boils. Cook for 2 minutes. Season and pour over courgettes.
Mix remaining cheese and breadcrumbs, sprinkle over sauce and bake at
200°C (400°F), mark 6 for 15 minutes until golden.

65 Calories per portion

Pasta Campania SERVES 4

Wholemeal spaghetti - *175g (6oz)*
Butter - *40g (1½ oz)*
Onion - *150g (5oz) sliced*
Garlic - *2 cloves, crushed*
Button mushrooms - *50g (2oz) sliced*
Salt *and freshly ground* **black pepper**
Cooked ham - *175g (6oz) cubed*
Tomatoes - *2, skinned and chopped*
Dried oregano - *5ml (1 tsp)*

Wholemeal flour - *30ml (2 tbsp)*
Fresh milk - *450ml (¾ pint)*
English Cheddar - *50g (2oz) grated*
Wholemeal breadcrumbs - *25g (1 oz)*

METHOD

1 Cook spaghetti as directed on the packet.

2 Melt 15g (½ oz) butter in a saucepan. Gently cook onion, garlic and mushrooms for 5 minutes. Season. Stir in ham, tomatoes and oregano.

3 Place remaining butter, flour and milk in a saucepan. Heat, stirring, until the sauce boils. Cook for 2 minutes. Remove from heat and add ham mixture and cheese. Place spaghetti on heatproof plates. Top with sauce, sprinkle with breadcrumbs and grill until golden.

55 Calories per portion

Tasty Pasta SERVES 4

Tagliatelle - *275g (10oz)*
Broccoli florets - *175g (6oz)*
Smoked bacon - *100g (4oz) rinded and chopped*
Garlic - *2 cloves, crushed*
Mushrooms - *75g (3oz) sliced*

Dried basil - *2.5ml (½ tsp)*
Plain flour - *40g (1½ oz)*
Fresh milk - *568ml (1 pint)*
Red Cheshire cheese - *50g (2 oz)*
Salt *and freshly ground* **black pepper**

METHOD

1 Cook pasta in boiling salted water as directed on the packet. Drain. Cook broccoli in boiling salted water for 5 minutes. Drain.

2 Dry fry bacon in a saucepan for 5 minutes, stirring frequently. Add garlic, mushrooms and basil. Cook for 2 minutes.

3 Stir in flour, gradually add milk and heat, stirring continuously until the sauce boils. Cook for 2 minutes. Remove from heat, crumble in most of the cheese and stir until melted. Season. Pour sauce over pasta and broccoli and serve sprinkled with remaining cheese.

455 Calories per portion

Gammon with Parsley & Mushroom Sauce SERVES 4

Gammon steaks - *4*
Tomatoes - *2, halved*
Butter - *15g (½ oz)*
Plain flour - *25g (1 oz)*
Fresh milk - *568ml (1 pint)*
Salt *and freshly ground* **black pepper**
Fresh parsley - *30ml (2 tbsp) chopped*
Button mushrooms - *175g (6oz) sliced*

METHOD

1 Grill gammon with tomatoes until tender. Keep warm.

2 Place butter, flour and milk in a saucepan. Heat, stirring continuously, until the sauce boils. Cook for 2 minutes. Season. Add parsley and mushrooms and simmer for 5 minutes. Serve with the gammon and tomatoes.

465 Calories per portion

Father's Ham Supper SERVES 4

Gammon steaks - *4*
Broccoli - *225g (8oz)*
Butter - *15g (½ oz)*
Wholemeal flour - *25g (1 oz)*
Fresh milk - *300ml (½ pint)*
Red Leicester cheese - *50g (2oz) grated*
Wholegrain mustard - *15ml (1 tbsp)*

METHOD

1 Grill ham and keep warm. Cook broccoli until tender. Keep warm.

2 Place butter, flour and milk in a saucepan. Heat, stirring, until the sauce boils. Cook for 2 minutes. Remove from heat and stir in cheese and mustard.

3 Transfer ham to serving plate. Top with sauce and broccoli and serve.

420 Calories per portion

Smoky Cauliflower Supper SERVES 4

Cauliflower - *1 medium, broken into florets*
Butter - *20g (¾ oz)*
Onion - *75g (3oz) chopped*
Plain flour - *25g (1 oz)*
Fresh milk - *300ml (½ pint)*
Salt *and freshly ground* **black pepper**
Prepared English mustard - *2.5ml (½ tsp)*

Smoked Cheddar cheese - *175g (6oz) grated*
Rye crispbread - *1, crushed*
Bacon rolls - *grilled, to garnish*

METHOD

1 Cook cauliflower in boiling salted water until tender.
Drain. Arrange in a shallow ovenproof dish.

2 Melt butter in a saucepan and gently cook
onion until soft. Stir in flour and milk and
heat, stirring, until sauce boils. Cook
for 2 minutes. Season. Remove from
heat, stir in mustard and most of cheese.
Pour over cauliflower.

3 Mix crispbread and remaining cheese.
Sprinkle over sauce and grill until golden.
Serve with bacon rolls.

---

395 Calories per portion

Leek & Ham Gougère SERVES 4

Leek - *1 large, washed and sliced*
Fresh milk - *300ml (½ pint)*
Bay leaf - *1*
Butter - *75g (3oz)*
Plain flour - *25g (1 oz) + 30ml (2 tbsp) milk*
Cooked ham - *100g (4oz) chopped*

Salt *and freshly ground* **black pepper**
Cold water - *150ml (¼ pint)*
Wholemeal flour - *65g (2½ oz)*
Eggs - *2 (size 3)*
English Cheddar cheese - *50g (2oz) grated*
Chopped parsley - *for garnish*

METHOD

1 Cook leek in milk with bay leaf until tender. Remove
bay leaf. Add 25g (1 oz) butter and plain flour.
Heat, stirring continuously, until the sauce boils.
Cook for 2 minutes. Add ham and season lightly.

2 Place water in saucepan. Add remaining butter
and bring to the boil. Remove pan from heat. Quickly
stir in wholemeal flour. Beat until smooth and mixture
leaves sides of the pan. Cool slightly.

3 Gradually add eggs, beating until smooth and glossy.
Add cheese. Spoon mixture around edge of a lightly
greased ovenproof dish. Pour sauce into the centre.
Bake at 220°C (425°F), mark 7 for 30 minutes until well
risen. Serve immediately sprinkled with parsley.

400 Calories per portion Ⓕ

Gourmet Liver SERVES 4

Lambs liver - *350g (12oz) sliced*
Seasoned wholemeal flour - *50g (2oz)*
Butter - *25g (1 oz)*
Garlic - *1 clove, crushed*
Back bacon - *4 rashers, chopped*
Onions - *225g (8oz) chopped*
Fresh milk - *300ml (½ pint)*
Dried mixed herbs - *5ml (1 tsp)*

METHOD
1 Coat liver in seasoned flour. Melt butter in a frying
pan, add liver and garlic and cook to your liking.
Remove from pan and keep warm.

2 Add bacon and onions to the pan. Cook for 5 minutes.
Stir in any remaining flour and gradually add milk.
Heat, stirring, until sauce boils. Add herbs and cook for
2 minutes. Serve with the liver.

285 Calories per portion

Creamed Liver SERVES 4

Butter - *15g (½ oz)*
Onions - *250g (9oz) chopped*
Chicken livers - *350g (12oz) cut in strips*
Salt *and freshly ground* **black pepper**
Eggs - *2 (size 3) hard boiled, chopped*
Paprika - *10ml (2 tsp)*
Fresh single cream - *150ml (¼ pint)*

METHOD
1 Melt butter in a large frying pan. Gently fry onion
until soft.

2 Season, add livers and cook a further 5 minutes.
Add remaining ingredients and re-heat gently, stirring
frequently. Serve immediately.

530 Calories per portion

Kidneys in Batter SERVES 4

Plain flour - *225g (8oz)*
Salt *and freshly ground* **black pepper**
Eggs - *2 (size 3) beaten*
Fresh milk - *568ml (1 pint)*
Butter - *25g (1 oz)*
Lambs kidneys - *8, cored and chopped*
Garlic - *1 clove, crushed*
Onion - *150g (5oz) chopped*
Button mushrooms - *100g (4oz) sliced*
Fresh double cream - *30ml (2 tbsp)*

METHOD

1 Sift flour and seasoning into a bowl. Gradually beat in eggs and milk to give a smooth batter.

2 Melt butter in a saucepan. Add kidneys, garlic, onion and mushrooms. Cook until tender. Add cream and season.

3 Lightly grease 8 Yorkshire pudding tins. Pour in batter and spoon kidney mixture into each. Bake at 200°C (400°F), mark 6 for 35 minutes until well risen. Serve immediately.

430 Calories per portion Ⓕ

Liver Peanut Casserole SERVES 4

Lambs liver - *450g (1 lb) cut in strips*
Seasoned wholemeal flour - *40g (1½ oz)*
Butter - *25g (1 oz)*
Onion - *150g (5oz) sliced*
Garlic - *1 clove, crushed*
Turmeric - *large pinch*

Chilli powder - *2.5ml (½ tsp)*
Soy sauce - *15ml (1 tbsp)*
Dry roasted peanuts - *50g (2oz)*
Fresh milk - *300ml (½ pint)*
Low fat natural yogurt - *60ml (4 tbsp)*

METHOD

1 Coat liver in seasoned flour. Melt butter in a saucepan, add onions and garlic and cook until soft.

2 Add liver, spices, soy sauce and peanuts and cook for 2 minutes. Add milk, cover and simmer for 5 minutes. Serve topped with yogurt.
N.B.
Omit peanuts if serving to young children.

Flans

460 Calories per portion Ⓕ

Herby Onion Quiche   SERVES 4

Butter - *75g (3oz)*
Wholemeal flour - *150g (5oz)*
Fresh milk - *200ml (7fl oz)*
Onion - *100g (4oz) chopped*
Red pepper - *1, de-seeded and diced*
Sage Derby cheese - *100g (4oz) grated*
Eggs - *2 (size 3), beaten*
Salt *and freshly ground* **black pepper**

METHOD

1 Rub 65g (2½ oz) butter into flour until it
resembles fine breadrumbs. Stir in 45ml (3 tbsp) milk
and bind together. Roll out and use to line a 20.5cm (8 inch)
metal flan ring.

2 Melt remaining butter in a saucepan. Add onion and
pepper and cook until tender. Place in base of flan.

3 Mix cheese, eggs and remaining milk. Season.
Pour into flan case and bake at 200°C (400°F),
mark 6 for 30 minutes until golden.

345 Calories per portion Ⓕ

Mackerel & Sweetcorn Flan   SERVES 6

Butter - *75g (3oz)*
Wholemeal flour - *175g (6oz)*
Fresh milk - *200ml (7fl oz)*
Smoked mackerel fillets - *175g (6oz)*
Canned sweetcorn - *100g (4oz)*
Eggs - *2 (size 3)*
Cottage cheese - *100g (4oz)*
Salt *and freshly ground* **black pepper**
Fresh parsley - *30ml (2 tbsp) chopped*

METHOD

1 Rub butter into flour until the mixture resembles fine
breadcrumbs. Mix to a dough with 45ml (3 tbsp) milk.
Roll out and use to line a 23cm (9 inch) metal flan tin.
Bake blind at 190°C (375°F), mark 5 for 10 minutes.

2 Skin and flake mackerel. Place in flan case with
sweetcorn. Beat eggs, cottage cheese and remaining
milk. Season lightly and pour over mackerel. Sprinkle
with parsley. Bake at the same temperature for
35 minutes until set.

Flans

395 Calories per portion Ⓕ

Creamy Sage & Onion Flan   SERVES 4

Butter - *90g (3½ oz)*
Wholemeal flour - *150g (5oz)*
Onion - *250g (9oz)*
Garlic - *1 clove, crushed*
Low fat curd cheese - *100g (4oz)*
Fresh milk - *150ml (¼ pint)*
Eggs - *2 (size 3) beaten*
Fresh sage - *15ml (1 tbsp) chopped*
Salt *and freshly ground* **black pepper**

METHOD

1 Rub 65g (2½ oz) butter into flour until it resembles fine breadcrumbs. Stir in 45ml (3 tbsp) water and bind together. Roll out and use to line a 18cm (7 inch) metal flan ring.

2 Melt remaining butter in a saucepan. Gently cook onion and garlic until soft. Arrange in base of flan case.

3 Blend curd cheese, milk, eggs and sage. Season lightly. Pour into flan case and bake at 200°C (400°F), mark 6 for 40 minutes until golden.

---

425 Calories per portion Ⓕ

Crunchy Spinach Flan   SERVES 4

Branflakes - *75g (3oz) crushed*
Granary flour - *75g (3oz)*
Sesame seeds - *15g (½ oz)*
Butter - *75g (3 oz) diced*
Fresh milk - *200ml (7fl oz)*
Low fat curd cheese - *75g (3oz)*
Eggs - *2 (size 3)*
Spinach - *75g (3oz) cooked*
Bacon - *2 rashers, cooked and chopped*

METHOD

1 Mix branflakes, flour and sesame seeds. Rub in butter until the mixture resembles fine breadcrumbs. Stir in 45ml (3 tbsp) milk and bind together. Roll out and use to line a 20.5cm (8 inch) metal flan ring. Bake blind at 190°C (375°F), mark 5 for 15 minutes.

2 Blend remaining milk, curd cheese, eggs, spinach and bacon. Pour into flan case and bake at same temperature for 40 minutes until golden.

305 Calories per portion

Perfect Potatoes

SERVES 4

Baking potatoes - *4×225g (8oz)*
Low fat yogurt - *150g (5oz)*
Hard boiled eggs - *2 (size 3) chopped*
Canned sweetcorn - *75g (3oz)*

English Cheddar cheese - *50g (2oz) grated*
Salt *and freshly ground* **black pepper**
Fresh chives - *30ml (2 tbsp) chopped*

MICROWAVE INSTRUCTIONS

1 Wash and dry potatoes. Prick skins all over.

2 Arrange potatoes on kitchen paper and cook on HIGH
for 18 minutes. Leave to stand for 5 minutes.

3 Cut a slice from the top of each potato.
Scoop out most of the flesh into a bowl.
Mix with remaining ingredients and spoon
back into the potato shells.

4 Stand in a shallow ovenproof
dish. Place under a hot grill for
several minutes until golden brown.

Timings are for a 600 watt oven.

---

345 Calories per portion Ⓕ

Cabbage Pie

SERVES 4

Cabbage leaves - *10 large*
Potatoes - *700g (1½ lb) cooked and mashed*
Runner beans - *100g (4oz) sliced*
Leeks - *2, washed and sliced*
Cabbage - *100g (4oz) sliced*
Eggs - *3 (size 3), beaten*
Fresh milk - *300ml (½ pint)*
English Cheddar cheese - *75g (3oz) grated*

Salt *and freshly ground* **black pepper**
Fresh sage - *30ml (2 tbsp) chopped*

METHOD

1 Remove tough stems from cabbage leaves. Cook in
boiling water until tender. Drain well.

2 Butter a shallow 25.5cm (10 inch) ovenproof dish.
Line with mashed potato, then overlapping cabbage leaves,
leaving them hanging over the edge.

3 Cook remaining vegetables in boiling salted water until
tender. Drain well and arrange over cabbage leaves.

4 Mix eggs, milk, cheese, seasoning and sage. Pour
over vegetables. Fold cabbage leaves over the top.
Bake at 190°C (375°F), mark 5 for 30 minutes.
Serve hot.

65 Calories per portion Ⓕ

Chequer-Board Pizza   SERVES 4

nion - *175g (6oz) chopped*
omatoes - *400g can*
ried basil - *5ml (1 tsp)*
lushrooms - *75g (3oz) sliced*
reen pepper - *1, de-seeded and diced*
elf-raising flour - *225g (8oz)*

Butter - *50g (2oz)*
Fresh milk - *100ml (4fl oz)*
Mozzarella - *75g (3oz) grated*
Sage Derby - *75g (3oz) grated*
Cotswold cheese - *75g (3oz) grated*
Anchovies - *1 can, drained*

METHOD

Simmer onion, tomatoes, basil, mushrooms and pepper ntil most of the liquid has evaporated.

Place flour in a bowl. Rub in butter until mixture esembles fine breadcrumbs. Add milk and mix to dough. Roll out to 28×18cm (11×7 inches), uilding up edges to form a rim. Place on a reased baking sheet. Bake at 220°C (425°F), ark 7 for 10 minutes.

Spread base with tomatoes. Arrange cheeses a chequered pattern, decorate with anchovies and ke a further 10 minutes.

0 Calories per portion

Vegetable Fluff   SERVES 4

lixed root vegetables - *900g (2 lb) cooked, diced*
earl barley - *75g (3oz) soaked then cooked*
egetable stock cube - *1*
resh milk - *450ml (¾ pint)*
ourgettes - *450g (1 lb) peeled and diced*
alt *and freshly ground* **black pepper**
round nutmeg - *large pinch*
ggs - *3 (size 3) separated*

METHOD

Place vegetables with barley in base of a deep 1 litre 2 pint) greased ovenproof dish. Dissolve stock cube 150ml (¼ pint) warm milk. Pour over vegetables.

Gently simmer courgettes in remaining milk with easoning and nutmeg until soft. Purée in a food rocessor or blender.

Beat egg yolks into courgette purée. Whisk whites ntil stiff and fold into purée. Pile on top of vegetables nd bake at 190°C (375°F), mark 5 for 40 minutes ntil risen and golden. Serve immediately.

otatoes, swede and carrots are a tasty combination.

365 Calories per portion*

Aubergine Fritters SERVES 4

Aubergines - *2 large, sliced*
Salt
Plain flour - *100g (4oz)*
Cayenne pepper - *large pinch*

Eggs - *2 (size 3) beaten*
Fresh milk - *150ml (¼ pint)*
Oil - *for deep frying*
Lemon wedges - *for serving*

METHOD

1 Place aubergine slices on a plate, sprinkle with salt. Leave for 10 minutes. Dry on kitchen paper, then turn over, sprinkle with salt, leave 10 minutes and dry on kitchen paper.

2 Sieve flour and pepper into a bowl. Make a well in the centre. Beat in eggs, gradually incorporating flour from the side of the well. Then slowly beat in milk to give a smooth batter. Add aubergine slices and leave for 15 minutes.

3 Heat oil in a deep fat fryer to 190°C (375°F). Lightly drain aubergine slices and fry for 2-3 minutes until golden. Drain well on kitchen paper. Serve immediately with lemon wedges.

*The amount of fat absorbed during cooking will vary and so the calorie value quoted is only a rough estimate.

330 Calories per portion

Blue Stilton Soufflé SERVES 4

Butter - *25g (1 oz)*
Plain flour - *30ml (2 tbsp)*
Fresh milk - *200ml (7 fl oz)*
Port - *30ml (2 tbsp)*

Eggs - *4 (size 3) separated*
Blue Stilton - *75g (3oz)*
Walnut pieces - *25g (1 oz) chopped*
Black pepper - *freshly ground*

METHOD

1 Grease a 1.4 litre (2½ pint) soufflé dish.

2 Melt butter in a large saucepan. Stir in flour and cook gently for 1 minute. Remove from heat. Gradually stir in milk and port. Bring to the boil and cook, stirring, for 2 minutes. Cool.

3 Beat yolks into sauce, one at a time. Stir in crumbled Stilton, ensuring it melts. Add walnuts. Season.

4 Whisk whites until they stand in soft peaks when the whisk is lifted. Fold a spoonful into the sauce with a metal spoon. Gently fold in remainder. Pour gently into the soufflé dish. Place on a baking sheet and bake at 180°C (350°F), mark 4 for 30 minutes until well risen. Serve immediately. There should be a hint of softness in the centre when eaten.

5 *Calories per portion*

Devilled Mushrooms
SERVES 4

utter - *20g (¾ oz)*
utton mushrooms - *175g (6oz) sliced*
ain flour - *15ml (1 tbsp)*
esh milk - *150ml (¼ pint)*
orcestershire sauce - *10ml (2 tsp)*

French mustard - *5ml (1 tsp)*
Tomato purée - *15ml (1 tbsp)*
Wholemeal toast - *4 slices buttered, to serve*
Fresh parsley - *chopped, for garnish*

ETHOD

Melt butter in a saucepan. Gently cook
ushrooms for 2 minutes.

Stir in flour, cook for 1 minute then
adually stir in remaining ingredients.
eat stirring continuously until sauce
ils. Cook for 2 minutes. Serve on
t toast, garnished with parsley.

5 *Calories per portion*

Curried Supper Eggs
SERVES 4

utter - *25g (1 oz)*
nion - *150g (5oz) sliced*
urry powder - *10ml (2 tsp)*
holemeal flour - *45ml (3 tbsp)*
esh milk - *450ml (¾ pint)*
ango chutney - *45ml (3 tbsp)*
ltanas - *25g (1 oz)*
rd boiled eggs - *4 (size 3)*
own rice - *to serve*

ETHOD

Melt butter in a saucepan. Add onion and curry
wder and cook gently until soft.

Stir in flour and cook for 2 minutes. Gradually add milk,
rring continuously until boiling. Add chutney and sultanas.
ver and simmer for 5 minutes.

Cut eggs in half, add to sauce and serve with rice.

415 Calories per portion

Pete's Pasta Salad SERVES 6

Pasta spirals - *225g (8oz)*
Broccoli florets - *225g (8oz)*
Double Gloucester cheese - *225g (8oz) cubed*
Red kidney beans - *425g can, drained*
Eating apple - *1, sliced*
Fresh soured cream - *150g (5oz)*
Apple juice - *30ml (2 tbsp)*
Fresh parsley - *30ml (2 tbsp) chopped*

METHOD

1 Cook pasta according to directions on the packet. Drain.

2 Cook broccoli in boiling salted water until just tender. Drain, refresh under cold running water. Drain.

3 Mix pasta, broccoli, cheese, kidney beans and apple in a serving bowl.

4 Beat soured cream, apple juice and parsley and serve with the salad.

385 Calories per portion

Autumn Cheese Salad SERVES 4

Sage Derby cheese - *225g (8oz) cubed*
Pineapple in natural juice - *225g can, drained*
Raisins - *50g (2oz)*
Red pepper - *½, de-seeded and diced*
Chinese leaves - *175g (6oz) shredded*
Walnut pieces - *25g (1 oz)*
Low fat natural yogurt - *150g (5oz)*
Wholegrain mustard - *10ml (2 tsp)*
Garlic - *1 clove, crushed*
Clear honey - *5ml (1 tsp)*
Chopped chives - *for garnish*

METHOD

1 Combine cheese, fruit, vegetables and nuts in a bowl.

2 Combine remaining ingredients, mix well and pour over the salad. Serve garnished with chives.

70 Calories per portion

Winter Salad

SERVES 4

Butter - *15g (½ oz)*
Plain flour - *20ml (4 tsp)*
Hard boiled eggs - *2 (size 3), yolks only*
Fresh milk - *300ml (½ pint)*
Malt vinegar - *15ml (1 tbsp)*
Salt *and* white pepper
Dry mustard - *2.5ml (½ tsp)*

Broccoli florets - *225g (8oz) blanched*
Cauliflower florets - *225g (8oz) blanched*
Spring onions - *6, sliced*

METHOD

1 Melt butter in a saucepan. Stir in flour
and cook gently for 1 minute. Remove
from the heat.

2 Sieve yolks and mix to a smooth paste
with flour/butter mixture. Gradually add
milk, stirring continuously. Return to heat and
simmer for 1 minute, stirring continuously. Cool,
then add vinegar and seasonings.

3 Mix broccoli, cauliflower and onions in a serving
bowl and serve dressing separately.

40 Calories per portion

Fruity Bean Salad

SERVES 4

Chickpeas - *415g can, drained and rinsed*
Red kidney beans - *220g can, drained and rinsed*
Bean sprouts - *100g (4oz)*
Radishes - *100g (4oz) sliced*
Carrots - *2, sliced*
Green pepper - *1, de-seeded and chopped*
Oranges - *2, segmented and chopped*
Green grapes - *100g (4oz) halved and seeded*
Eating apple - *1, cored and chopped*
Ground ginger - *large pinch*
Low fat natural yogurt - *300g (10oz)*
Fresh mint - *30ml (2 tbsp) chopped*
Sugar - *2.5ml (½ tsp)*

METHOD

1 Mix chickpeas, kidney beans, vegetables and fruit.
Chill.

2 Blend ginger with a little yogurt. Stir in remaining
yogurt, mint and sugar. Chill. Serve with the salad.

550 Calories per portion

Melting Cheese & Basil Pie   SERVES 4

Eggs - *4 (size 3)*
Fresh milk - *568ml (1 pint)*
Thin slices bread - *8*
Chopped tomatoes - *2 × 397g cans*
Fresh parsley - *30ml (2 tbsp) chopped*
Fresh basil - *30ml (2 tbsp) chopped*
Mozzarella cheese - *225g (8oz) thinly sliced*

METHOD

1 Grease 1.25 litre (1¼ pint) ovenproof dish.

2 Beat eggs and milk and coat 3 slices bread.
Arrange in base of the dish. Pour over one third
tomatoes, sprinkle with some parsley and basil and
top with one third of cheese. Keeping back a slice of
cheese, repeat the layering, finishing with tomatoes
and herbs.

3 Bake at 200°C (400°F), mark 6 for 30 minutes. Top
with cheese and return to oven until cheese has melted.

310 Calories per portion Ⓕ

Storecupboard Pizza   SERVES 4

Pizza base mix - *150g packet*
Fresh milk - *to make up mix*
Spaghetti sauce - *½ × 320g jar*
Frozen mixed vegetables - *100g (4oz)*
Sliced mushrooms - *213g can, drained*
English Cheddar cheese - *100g (4oz) grated*

METHOD

1 Make up pizza base as directed on the packet —
using milk instead of water. Knead well on a floured
surface.

2 Roll out a 20.5cm (8 inch) circle, place on a baking
sheet and leave to prove in a warm place for 25 minutes.

3 Mix sauce, vegetables and most of mushrooms.
Spoon over base, top with cheese and remaining
mushrooms. Bake at 220°C (425°F), mark 7 for
25 minutes until risen and golden.

) Calories per portion 🅕

Gloucester Cheese Pudding

SERVES 4

ouble **Gloucester cheese** - *225g (8oz) grated*
oasted **peanuts** - *50g (2oz) chopped*
holemeal bread - *8 slices*
utter - *25g (1 oz) softened*
esh parsley - *15ml (1 tbsp) chopped*
ggs - *3 (size 3)*
esh milk - *450ml (¾ pint)*
holegrain mustard - *5ml (1 tsp)*
alt *and freshly ground* **black pepper**

ETHOD

Mix 100g (4oz) cheese with the nuts and make
andwiches with the bread and butter. Remove crusts
d cut into triangles. Arrange in a greased 1.1 litre
pint) ovenproof dish. Sprinkle with remaining cheese
d parsley.

Whisk eggs, milk, mustard and seasoning.
ur over bread and leave to stand for 30 minutes.

Bake at 180°C (350°F), mark 4 for 40-45 minutes
til set and golden.

not add peanuts if serving to young children.

) Calories per portion 🅕

Cheesy Loaf

SERVES 4

ng grain **rice** - *175g (6oz)*
ozzarella **cheese** - *75g (3oz) cubed*
ncashire **cheese** - *75g (3oz) grated*
gg - *1 (size 3), beaten*
esh **milk** - *225ml (8fl oz)*

Mixed herbs - *5ml (1 tsp)*
Red or green pepper - *for garnish*

ETHOD

Cook rice as directed on the packet. Drain.

Mix rice, both cheeses, egg, milk and herbs. Spoon into a
0g (1 lb) loaf tin. Bake at 190°C (375°F), mark 5 for 15-20 minutes
until firm. Turn out and garnish with chopped peppers.

435 Calories per portion

Cheese Cannelloni SERVES 2

Fresh lasagne - *4 sheets*
Cottage cheese - *175g (6oz)*
English Cheddar cheese - *100g (4oz) grated*
Fresh parsley - *15ml (1 tbsp) chopped*
Egg yolk - *1 (size 3)*
Salt *and freshly ground* **black pepper**
Cornflour - *10ml (2 tsp)*
Tomato juice - *175g (6fl oz)*
Worcestershire sauce - *10ml (2 tsp)*

MICROWAVE INSTRUCTIONS

1 Place pasta in a bowl, cover with boiling water and cook on HIGH for 2 minutes. Drain pasta on kitchen paper.

2 Mix cheeses, parsley, egg yolk and seasoning. Divide between pasta, roll up and place in a dish.

3 Blend cornflour, tomato juice and Worcestershire sauce. Cook on HIGH for 3 minutes, stirring every minute.

4 Pour half sauce over pasta. Cover and cook on MEDIUM for 5 minutes. Leave to stand for 3 minutes. Serve with remaining sauce.

Timings are for a 600 watt oven.

315 Calories per portion

Lasagne Rolls SERVES 4

Cooked spinach - *100g (4oz) drained and chopped*
Cottage cheese - *225g (8oz) drained*
Egg - *1 (size 3) beaten*
Salt *and freshly ground* **black pepper**
Wholemeal lasagne - *8 sheets, almost cooked*
Butter - *15g (½ oz)*
Wholemeal flour - *25g (1 oz)*
Fresh milk - *300ml (½ pint)*
Red Leicester cheese - *50g (2oz) grated*

METHOD

1 Mix spinach, cottage cheese and egg. Season and roll up in lasagne sheets. Place any remaining mixture in the base of a shallow ovenproof dish and arrange lasagne on top.

2 Place butter, flour and milk in a saucepan. Heat, stirring continuously until sauce boils. Cook for 2 minutes. Remove from heat, stir in cheese and pour around lasagne. Bake at 190°C (375°F), mark 5 for 20 minutes to heat through.

95 *Calories per portion*

Pasta & Cauliflower Cheese SERVES 4

Cauliflower - *1 medium*
Wholemeal pasta spirals - *100g, cooked*
Wholemeal flour - *45ml (3 tbsp)*
Butter - *15g (½ oz)*
Fresh milk - *300ml (½ pint)*
English Cheddar cheese - *100g (4oz) grated*
Salt *and freshly ground* black pepper
Wheatgerm - *15ml (1 tbsp)*

METHOD

Break cauliflower into florets. Cook in boiling salted water for 8 minutes. Drain and arrange in the base of an overproof dish with the pasta.

Place flour, butter and milk in a saucepan. Heat, stirring continuously until the sauce boils. Cook for 2 minutes. Remove from heat, stir in most of cheese, season and pour over pasta.

Mix remaining cheese and wheatgerm, sprinkle over the top and grill until golden.

55 *Calories per portion*

Wheat & Cauliflower Casserole SERVES 4

Whole wheat grains - *225g (8oz)*
Butter - *25g (1 oz)*
Onion - *1 small, sliced*
Garlic - *1 clove, crushed*
Fresh milk - *900ml (1½ pints)*
Vegetable stock cube - *1*
Lemon - *1, rind only*
Small potatoes - *450g (1 lb) quartered*
Courgettes - *2, sliced*
Cauliflower - *½, cut in florets*
English Cheddar cheese - *50g (2oz) grated*

METHOD

Soak wheat grains overnight. Drain.

Heat half butter in a large saucepan. Add onion and garlic and cook until soft. Add wheat and cook for 5 minutes. Add milk, crumbled stock cube, lemon rind and potatoes. Cook for 15 minutes.

Fry courgettes in remaining butter until golden. Add to saucepan with the cauliflower. Cook for 15-20 minutes. Sprinkle with cheese and serve.

445 Calories per portion **F**

Leek & Carrot Medley

SERVES 4

Leeks - *900g (2 lb) trimmed, thickly sliced*
Carrots - *675g (1½ lb) thickly sliced*
Vegetable stock - *450ml (¾ pint)*
Fresh milk - *450ml (¾ pint)*
Cashew nuts - *50g (2 oz) toasted*
Plain flour - *40g (1½ oz)*
Butter - *25g (1 oz)*
Sage Derby cheese - *75g (3oz) grated*
Salt *and freshly ground* **black pepper**
Fresh wholemeal breadcrumbs - *40g (1½ oz)*

METHOD

1 Place vegetables and stock in a saucepan. Bring to the boil, cover and simmer for 10 minutes. Drain, reserve liquid and make up to 900ml (1½ pints) with milk. Arrange vegetables in a shallow ovenproof dish. Keep warm.

2 Place flour, butter and milk in a saucepan. Heat, stirring, until the sauce boils. Cook for 2 minutes. Remove from the heat, season and stir in cheese. Pour over the vegetables, sprinkle with breadcrumbs and grill until golden.

275 Calories per portion **F**

Vegetable Casserole

SERVES 4

Butter - *25g (1 oz)*
Onions - *300g (11oz) sliced*
Garlic - *2 cloves, crushed*
Carrots - *225g (8oz) sliced*
Celery - *4 sticks, sliced*
Potato - *225g (8oz) peeled and cubed*
Paprika - *30ml (2 tbsp)*
Red kidney beans - *220g can, drained*
Vegetable stock - *300ml (½ pint)*
Fresh milk - *450ml (¾ pint)*
Tomato purée - *30ml (2 tbsp)*
Cornflour - *30ml (2 tbsp)*

METHOD

1 Melt butter in a saucepan, add vegetables and paprika and cook gently for 5 minutes.

2 Add kidney beans, stock, most of the milk and tomato purée. Bring to the boil and simmer for 30 minutes.

3 Blend cornflour with remaining milk, add to saucepan and bring to the boil, stirring continuously. Cook for 2 minutes before serving.

435 Calories per portion **F**

Stuffed Aubergines SERVES 4

Aubergines - *2, halved lengthwise*
Parşnip - *1, peeled and diced*
Carrot - *1, peeled and diced*
Courgettes - *2, diced*
Butter - *40g (1½ oz)*
Salt *and freshly ground* **black pepper**
Dried mixed herbs - *5ml (1 tsp)*

Tomato purée - *15ml (1 tbsp)*
Brown rice - *50g (2oz), cooked*
Aduki beans - *½×430g can, drained*
Plain flour - *25g (1 oz)*
Fresh milk - *568ml (1 pint)*
Mozzarella cheese - *100g (4oz)*

METHOD

1 Simmer aubergine halves gently in water for 3 minutes. Drain and cool. Scoop out flesh.

2 Gently fry remaining vegetables in 25g (1 oz) butter until soft. Season. Stir in herbs, tomato purée, aubergine, rice and beans. Spoon into cases. Place in an ovenproof dish.

3 Place flour, remaining butter and milk in a saucepan. Heat, stirring, until the sauce boils. Cook for 2 minutes. Remove from heat, season and add cheese. Pour over aubergines, cover and cook at 190°C (375°F), mark 5 for 30 minutes.

---

535 Calories per portion **F**

Vegetable & Nut Cobbler SERVES 6

Butter - *115g (4½ oz)*
Cauliflower florets - *350g (12oz)*
Baby onions - *6*
Carrots - *175g (6oz) sliced*
Parsnip - *150g (5oz) sliced*
Green beans - *175g (6oz) sliced*
Butter beans - *397g can, drained*
Vegetable stock cube - *1*
Fresh milk - *568ml (1 pint)*

Black pepper *freshly ground*
Wholemeal self-raising flour - *225g (8oz)*
Baking powder - *10ml (2 tsp)*
Walnut pieces - *50g (2oz)*
Red Leicester cheese - *100g (4oz) grated*

METHOD

1 Melt 15g (½ oz) butter in a large saucepan. Add vegetables, cover and cook gently for 10 minutes.

2 Add butter beans, stock cube and 450ml (¾ pint) milk. Transfer to a casserole, cover and bake at 220°C (425°F), mark 7 for 15 minutes.

3 Sift flour and baking powder, rub in remaining butter and add nuts. Stir in remaining milk and mix to a soft dough. Roll out to 1cm (½ inch) thick. Cut into 12.

4 Remove casserole from oven. Sprinkle with cheese and arrange scones on top. Brush with milk. Bake at 180°C (350°F), mark 4 for 15 minutes, until golden.

440 Calories per portion Ⓕ

Chilli Pancakes
SERVES 4

Plain flour - *100g (4oz)*
Egg - *1 (size 3)*
Fresh milk - *300ml (½ pint)*
Butter - *for frying*
Onion - *75g (3oz) chopped*
Garlic - *1 clove, crushed*
Red kidney beans - *425g can, drained*

Baked beans - *425g can*
Tomatoes - *397g can*
Chilli powder - *10ml (2 tsp)*
Frozen green beans - *225g (8oz)*
Yellow pepper - *1, de-seeded and chopped*
Red Leicester cheese - *50g (2oz) grated*

METHOD
1 Place flour in a bowl. Break egg in the centre. Beat well, gradually adding milk to give a smooth batter.

2 Lightly brush base of 18cm (7 inch) frying pan with butter. When hot, pour in 45ml (3 tbsp) batter, tilting to cover the base. Cook until pancake moves freely, turn and cook until golden. Repeat to make 8 pancakes.

3 Place onion, garlic, beans, tomatoes and chilli powder in a saucepan. Simmer for 15 minutes. Add green beans and pepper and cook until thick.

4 Divide between pancakes, fold into triangles, place in base of shallow ovenproof dish, sprinkle with cheese and grill until golden.

---

485 Calories per portion

Naan Parcels
SERVES 6

Egg - *1 (size 3) beaten*
Salt - *2.5ml (½ tsp)*
Baking powder - *15ml (1 tbsp)*
Sugar - *5ml (1 tsp)*
Dried yeast - *7.5ml (1½ tsp)*
Butter - *50g (2oz) melted*
Low fat natural yogurt - *60ml (4 tbsp)*

Strong plain flour - *450g (1 lb)*
Fresh milk - *200ml (7fl oz)*
White cabbage - *200g (7oz) shredded*
Carrots - *4, peeled and grated*
Raisins - *50g (2oz)*
Hazelnuts - *25g (1 oz) halved and toasted*
Low fat hazelnut yogurt - *300g (10oz)*

METHOD
1 Beat egg, salt, baking powder, sugar, yeast, half butter and natural yogurt. Stir in flour, add milk and knead until smooth. Cover and leave in warm place until doubled in size.

2 Knead for 1 minute, divide into 6 balls, flatten and roll into teardrop shapes. Rest for 5-10 minutes.

3 Brush each side with remaining butter and grill for 1 minute on each side. Leave to cool.

4 Mix remaining ingredients thoroughly, cut naan in half and fill pocket. Serve immediately.

525 Calories per portion

Cheese Stir-Fry
SERVES 2

Butter - *15g (½ oz)*
Garlic - *1 clove, crushed*
Spring onions - *2*
Cabbage - *175g (6oz) shredded*
Bean sprouts - *225g (8oz)*
Sweetcorn - *100g (4oz)*
Red pepper - *½, de-seeded and sliced*

Orange juice - *45ml (3 tbsp)*
Soy sauce - *45ml (3 tbsp)*
Red Leicester cheese - *150g (5oz) cubed*
Boiled rice - *to serve*

METHOD

1 Melt butter. Fry garlic, spring onions and cabbage for 30 seconds, stirring continuously.

2 Add bean sprouts, sweetcorn and red pepper. Cook, stirring, for 2 minutes. Stir in orange juice and soy sauce, remove from heat and stir in cheese. Serve immediately with rice.

---

200 Calories per portion Ⓕ

Tortillas
SERVES 4

Egg - *1 (size 3)*
Fresh milk - *300ml (½ pint)*
Cornmeal flour - *50g (2oz) sieved*
Wholemeal flour - *50g (2oz) sieved*
Cornflour - *15ml (1 tbsp)*

Salt - *pinch*
Butter - *melted, for frying*

METHOD

1 Beat egg until fluffy. Add milk, then flours, cornflour and salt. Mix until smooth. Stand for 10 minutes.

2 Heat a 15cm (6 inch) thick based frying pan, brush with butter and place over medium heat. Pour in sufficient batter to almost cover the base, spreading with the back of a spoon. Cook for 3-4 minutes, turning once. Keep warm in oven.

3 Fill tortillas with a chilli meat mixture or any savoury filling — tuna, stir fried vegetables or chicken.

515 Calories per portion

Kiwi and Ginger Castles SERVES 4

Wholemeal self-raising flour - *75g (3oz)*
Self-raising flour - *75g (3oz)*
Baking powder - *5ml (1 tsp)*
Ground ginger - *5ml (1 tsp)*
Butter - *75g (3oz)*
Caster sugar - *25g (1 oz)*
Fresh milk - *100ml (4fl oz)*
Egg - *1 (size 3), beaten*
Crystallised ginger - *25g (1 oz) diced*

Fresh double cream - *150ml (¼ pint)*
Ginger wine - *10ml (2 tsp)*
Kiwi fruit - *1, peeled and sliced*

METHOD

1 Sieve flours, baking powder and ginger. Return bran to the bowl. Rub in butter, add sugar and beat in milk and egg.

2 Arrange slices of ginger in base of 8 individual, greased, metal moulds. Fill each ¾ full, cover with greased foil, tie securely with string and steam in a saucepan of simmering water for 1 hour. Unmould and serve with lightly whipped cream flavoured with ginger wine. Decorate with slices of kiwi fruit.

325 Calories per portion

Banana Bread Pudding SERVES 4

Wholemeal bread - *5 medium slices*
Butter - *20g (¾ oz) approx.*
Demerara sugar - *10ml (2 tsp)*
Cinnamon - *2.5ml (½ tsp)*
Dried apricots - *50g (2oz), soaked*
Bananas - *2 medium, sliced*
Raisins - *25g (1 oz)*
Eggs - *2 (size 3)*
Fresh milk - *450ml (¾ pint)*

METHOD

1 Remove crusts and thinly spread bread with butter. Cut each slice into 4 squares. Mix sugar and cinnamon.

2 Chop apricots and mix with bananas and raisins. Place half in a 1.1 litre (2 pint) greased ovenproof dish. Sprinkle with a third of cinnamon sugar. Cover with half the bread, remaining apricot mixture and another third of sugar. Top with remaining bread — butter side up.

3 Beat eggs and milk, slowly pour over the bread and sprinkle with remaining sugar. Bake at 180°C (350°F), mark 4 for 35-40 minutes.

235 Calories per portion

Apple and Cheese Pudding SERVES 4

Eating apples - *450g (1 lb) sliced*
Butter - *20g (¾ oz)*
Vanilla essence - *few drops*
Medium fat curd cheese - *100g (4oz)*
Fresh milk - *150ml (¼ pint)*
Eggs - *2 (size 3) beaten*
Caster sugar - *25g (1 oz)*

METHOD

1 Cook apples gently in butter until slightly soft. Add vanilla essence and place in a buttered ovenproof dish.

2 Blend curd cheese with a little milk. Beat in remaining milk, eggs and sugar. Pour over apple. Bake at 190°C (375°F), mark 5 for 25 minutes. Serve hot.

460 Calories per portion ⑤

Wholemeal Steamed Marmalade Pud SERVES 4

PUDDING
Orange - *1*
Butter - *75g (3oz)*
Caster sugar - *75g (3oz)*
Eggs - *2 (size 3), beaten*

Wholemeal S.R. flour - *75g (3oz)*
Dark marmalade - *30ml (2 tbsp)*
Fresh milk - *45ml (3 tbsp)*

ORANGE SAUCE
Cornflour - *25g (1 oz)*
Sugar - *25g (1 oz)*
Fresh milk - *450ml (¾ pint)*
Orange - *1, grated rind and juice*

METHOD

1 Grease a 900ml (1½ pint) basin and line base with greased paper.

2 Grate orange rind. Remove pith, slice orange thinly and use to line base and sides of basin.

3 Cream butter and sugar until fluffy. Beat in eggs. Gently fold in flour, marmalade, orange rind and milk. Pour into basin. Cover with a layer of greased foil. Tie securely with string.

4 Place on an upturned pyrex saucer in a saucepan, filled with boiling water to reach halfway up the basin. Steam for 2 hours, topping up with boiling water as required.

5 Blend cornflour and sugar with 30ml (2tbsp) milk. Heat remaining milk and blend with cornflour. Return to pan and heat stirring until boiling. Cook for 2 minutes. Stir in orange rind and juice. Serve with the pudding.

360 Calories per portion **F**

Coconut Crunch SERVES 6

Plain flour - *175g (6oz)*
Salt - *pinch*
Butter - *100g (4oz)*
Eggs - *2 (size 3) separated*
Sugar - *50g (2oz)*
Fresh milk - *150ml (¼ pint)*
Almond essence - *few drops*
Lemon essence - *few drops*
Desiccated coconut - *75g (3oz)*

METHOD

1 Sift flour and salt into a bowl. Rub in 75g (3oz) butter and mix to a soft dough with 45-60ml (3-4tbsp) water. Roll out and use to line a 20.5cm (8 inch) flan dish. Cut trimmings into star shapes.

2 Whisk egg yolks, sugar and milk. Add 25g (1 oz) melted butter, essences and coconut. Whisk egg whites until stiff and fold into the mixture. Pour into pastry case and decorate with pastry stars. Bake at 180°C (350°F), mark 4 for 25-30 minutes until set. Serve hot or cold.

405 Calories per portion

Tapioca Orange Pudding SERVES 4

Fresh milk - *568ml (1 pint)*
Oranges - *2 large*
Tapioca - *50g (2oz)*
Desiccated coconut - *75g (3oz)*
Allspice - *pinch*
Caster sugar - *25g (1 oz)*
Orange liqueur - *30ml (2 tbsp)*
Fresh single cream - *150ml (¼ pint)*

METHOD

1 Pour milk into a saucepan. Pare zest from oranges and add to pan. Bring to the boil, remove from heat and leave for 1 hour. Remove zest.

2 Add tapioca, 50g (2oz) coconut and allspice to milk. Bring to the boil. Simmer for 15 minutes until thick, stirring occasionally.

3 Remove peel and pith from oranges. Divide into segments and reserve some for decoration. Chop remainder and add to tapioca with sugar, liqueur and cream. Reheat gently. Pour into serving dishes.

4 Toast remaining coconut, sprinkle over tapioca and decorate with orange segments.

405 Calories per portion

Apricot Bread Pudding SERVES 4

Wholemeal bread - *8 medium thick slices*
Dried apricots - *75g (3oz) chopped*
Sultanas - *50g (2oz)*
Clear honey - *30ml (2 tbsp)*
Eggs - *2 (size 3)*
Fresh milk - *568ml (1 pint)*
Lemon - *½, grated rind only*
Mixed spice - *2.5ml (½ tsp)*

METHOD

1 Cut bread into triangles. Place half in the base of an ovenproof dish. Sprinkle half apricots and sultanas over the bread then drizzle over half the honey. Layer with remaining bread, fruit and honey.

2 Beat eggs, milk, lemon rind and spice. Pour slowly over bread and leave to stand for 15 minutes. Bake at 180°C (350°F), mark 4 for 40 minutes until lightly brown. Serve with custard.

415 Calories per portion

Raspberry Bread Pudding SERVES 6

Fresh milk - *568ml (1 pint)*
Fresh whipping cream - *150ml (¼ pint)*
Cinnamon stick - *7.5cm (3 inch)*
White bread - *6 medium thick slices*
Butter - *25g (1 oz) approx.*
Eggs - *3 (size 3) + 2 (size 3) yolks*

Sugar - *75g (3oz)*
Vanilla essence - *5ml (1 tsp)*
Raspberries - *225g (8oz)*

METHOD

1 Gently heat milk, cream and cinnamon stick until bubbles appear around the edge of the pan. Leave to stand.

2 Spread each slice of bread with butter and place buttered side up in a greased 1.1 litre (2 pint) ovenproof dish.

3 Beat eggs, yolks, sugar and essence. Remove cinnamon stick from the milk. Stir milk into egg mixture. Pour slowly over bread.

4 Place dish in a roasting tin half filled with water. Bake at 190°C (375°F), mark 5 for 45-50 minutes until set. Serve with raspberries.

190 Calories per portion

Fresh Strawberry Savarin SERVES 6

Fresh yeast - *15g (½ oz)*
Fresh milk - *150ml (¼ pint) warmed*
Plain flour - *175g (6oz) sieved*
Eggs - *2 (size 3)*
Caster sugar - *15g (½ oz)*

Clear honey - *45ml (3 tbsp)*
Dark rum - *to taste*
Strawberries - *225g (8oz)*
Fresh cream - *to serve*

METHOD

1 Grease and flour a 900ml (1½ pint) ring mould.

2 Cream yeast with a little milk. Add remaining milk.

3 Place flour in a bowl, make a well in the centre and add milk. Sprinkle with a little flour, cover and leave until frothy.

4 Whisk eggs and sugar until thick. Beat into yeast mixture. Pour into ring mould, cover and leave to rise for 10 minutes. Bake at 220°C (425°F), mark 7 for 30 minutes. Turn onto a wire rack to cool.

5 Warm honey with a 45ml (3 tbsp) water. Add rum. Place savarin on a serving plate, pour over rum syrup while still warm. Serve with strawberries and cream.

235 Calories per portion **F**

Pancake Ribbons SERVES 4

Plain wholemeal flour - *50g (2oz)*
Plain flour - *50g (2oz)*
Egg - *1 (size 3)*
Fresh milk - *300ml (½ pint)*
Butter - *for cooking pancakes*

Orange juice - *150ml (¼ pint)*
Orange - *1, grated zest only*
Orange liqueur - *30ml (2 tbsp)*
Clear honey - *15ml (1 tbsp)*

METHOD

1 Sieve flours into a bowl, returning bran to the bowl. Break in egg. Gradually beat in half the milk to give a creamy batter. Stir in remaining milk.

2 Heat a little butter in an 18cm (7 inch) non stick frying pan. When hot, pour in 45ml (3 tbsp) batter, tilting to cover the base. Cook until pancake moves freely, turn and cook until golden. Make 8 pancakes, stacking them in a pile. Roll up and slice into 1cm (½ inch) ribbons.

3 Place remaining ingredients in a saucepan. Bring to the boil, simmer for 1 minute.

4 Divide ribbons between 4 heated plates and coat with sauce. Serve immediately.

Hot Desserts

295 Calories per portion

Pasta Fruit Pudding SERVES 6

Glacé cherries - *50g (2oz)*
Fresh milk - *900ml (1½ pint)*
Quick cook pasta bows - *150g (5oz)*
Sultanas - *50g (2oz)*
Soft dark brown sugar - *25g (1 oz)*
Flaked almonds - *50g (2oz) toasted*
Grated nutmeg - *1.25ml (¼ tbsp)*

METHOD

1 Wash and halve the cherries.

2 Place milk in a saucepan and bring to the boil.

3 Add pasta, sultanas, sugar and cherries.
Simmer for 10 minutes. Add almonds and nutmeg.
Reheat and serve immediately.

*NB: Do not add nuts if
serving to young children*

300 Calories per portion 🅕

Sweet Pizza SERVES 6

Wholemeal self-raising flour - *225g (8oz)*
Salt - *2.5ml (½ tsp)*
Butter - *50g (2oz)*
Caster sugar - *25g (1 oz)*
Fresh milk - *150ml (¼ pint)*
Peaches in natural juice - *410g can*
Almonds - *50g (2oz)*
Arrowroot or cornflour - *15ml (1 tbsp)*

METHOD

1 Sift flour and salt into a bowl. Rub in butter and stir
in sugar. Add milk all at once and mix to a soft dough.
Roll out to an 18cm (7 inch) circle. Place on a non stick
baking sheet and bake at 220°C (425°F), mark 7 for
15 minutes.

2 Drain peaches, reserving juice, and arrange
over pizza base. Sprinkle with almonds. Blend
arrowroot and peach juice in a saucepan.
Heat until thick and spoon over peaches.

3 Return to oven for 10 minutes. Serve hot
with custard or fresh cream.

73

385 Calories per portion Ⓕ

Rhubarb Flan   SERVES 4

Wholemeal flour - *50g (2oz)*
Plain flour - *50g (2oz)*
Mixed spice - *2.5ml (½ tsp)*
Butter - *50g (2oz)*
Wholemeal breadcrumbs - *25g (1 oz)*
Rhubarb - *225g (8oz) cooked*
Sugar - *40g (1½ oz)*
Medium fat curd cheese - *225g (8oz)*
Eggs - *2 (size 3)*

METHOD

1 Sieve flours and mixed spice, returning bran to the bowl. Rub in butter until mixture resembles fine breadcrumbs. Add 45ml (3 tbsp) water and mix to a dough. Roll out and line a 15cm (6 inch) flan dish. Bake blind at 200°C (400°F), mark 6 for 10 minutes.

2 Sprinkle half breadcrumbs into flan case. Top with rhubarb and sugar. Whisk together cheese and eggs, spoon over rhubarb and sprinkle with remaining crumbs. Return to oven for a further 35 minutes until set.

230 Calories per portion

Cardamom Milk Tart   SERVES 6

Butter - *75g (3oz)*
Plain flour - *100g (4oz)*
Fresh milk - *300ml (½ pint)*
Cardamom pods - *3*
Cinnamon stick - *½*

Caster sugar - *25g (1 oz)*
Baking powder - *2.5ml (½ tsp)*
Cornflour - *10ml (2 tsp)*
Eggs - *2 (size 3) separated*
Ground cinnamon - *pinch*

METHOD

1 Rub 50g (2oz) butter into flour. Mix to a soft dough with 30-45ml (2-3tbsp) water. Roll out and use to line a 18cm (7 inch) flan ring. Bake blind at 200°C (400°F), mark 6 for 15 minutes.

2 Place milk in a saucepan with cardamom and cinnamon. Bring to the boil, remove from heat and leave for 15 minutes. Remove spices.

3 Mix sugar, baking powder, cornflour, milk, yolks and remaining butter in a saucepan and cook until thickened. Cool.

4 Whisk whites until soft, fold into custard. Pour into pastry case, sprinkle with cinnamon and bake at 180°C (350°F), mark 4 for 30 minutes. Serve hot or cold.

280 Calories per portion Ⓕ

St George's Tart   SERVES 4

Butter - *40g (1½ oz)*
Caster sugar - *65g (2½ oz)*
Egg yolk - *1 (size 3)*
Self-raising flour - *100g (4oz) sieved*

Rhubarb - *225g (8oz), washed and sliced*
Custard powder - *7.5ml (½ tbsp)*
Fresh milk - *200ml (7fl oz)*

METHOD

1 Cream butter and 25g (1 oz) sugar. Beat in yolk. Stir in flour and 45ml (3tbsp) milk to give a soft dough. Knead until smooth. Chill for 45 minutes. Roll out and use ⅔ to line a 15cm (6 inch) flan tin. Use remainder to make 8 × 2cm (¾ inch) strips.

2 Heat rhubarb and 25g (1 oz) sugar until sugar dissolves. Cover and simmer for 5 minutes. Drain.

3 Blend remaining sugar and custard powder with a little milk. Bring remaining milk to the boil and pour onto custard powder. Return to pan and heat, stirring, until sauce boils. Cook for 2 minutes

4 Spread custard in base of flan, top with rhubarb and decorate with pastry stips. Bake at 190°C (375°F), mark 5 for 40 minutes until golden.

---

245 Calories per portion Ⓕ

Curd Tart   SERVES 6

Plain wholemeal flour - *65g (2½ oz)*
Plain flour - *65g (2½ oz)*
Butter - *65g (2½ oz)*
Fresh milk - *30ml (2 tbsp)*
Medium fat curd cheese - *175g (6oz)*

Ground cinnamon - *2.5ml (½ tsp)*
Egg - *1 (size 3) beaten*
Caster sugar - *25g (1 oz)*
Lemon - *1, sliced for decoration*

METHOD

1 Place flours in a bowl. Rub in butter until mixture resembles fine breadcrumbs. Mix to a soft dough with 30ml (2tbsp) water. Roll out and line an 18cm (7 inch) flan ring. Bake blind at 200°C (400°F), mark 6 for 15 minutes.

2 Beat cheese with milk and cinnamon. Whisk egg and sugar until pale and thick. Gradually beat into cheese. Pour into pastry case. Bake at 190°C (375°F), mark 5 for 20 minutes until set. Decorate with lemon slices.

Hot Desserts

185 Calories per portion

Baked Rice Custard SERVES 6

Pudding rice - *50g (2oz)*
Eggs - *3 (size 3) beaten*
Sugar - *50g (2oz)*
Vanilla essence - *2.5ml (½ tsp)*
Fresh milk - *568ml (1 pint)*
Sultanas - *40g (1½ oz)*
Ground nutmeg - *pinch*

METHOD

1 Cook rice in boiling water for 10 minutes.
Drain well.

2 Beat eggs, sugar, essence and milk in a basin.
Add rice and sultanas. Pour into an ovenproof dish.
Sprinkle with nutmeg. Stand dish in a roasting tin
and fill with water to come half way up the sides
of the dish. Bake at 170°C (325°F), mark 3
for 1½ hours or until set.

165 Calories per portion

Souffléd Pink Grapefruit SERVES 4

Pink grapefruit - *2*
Arrowroot - *10ml (2 tsp)*
Sugar - *40g (1½ oz)*
Dry Vermouth - *30ml (2 tbsp)*
Eggs - *2 (size 3) separated*

Plain flour - *25ml (1½ tbsp)*
Fresh milk - *150ml (¼ pint)*
Vanilla essence - *2.5ml (½ tsp)*
Icing sugar - *5ml (1 tsp)*

METHOD

1 Cut grapefruit in half and scoop out flesh. Purée,
then sieve flesh. Blend with arrowroot, 15g (½ oz)
sugar and 15ml (1tbsp) Vermouth. Heat in a saucepan
until thick and glossy. Keep warm.

2 Whisk yolks and 15g (½ oz) sugar until thick. Stir in flour.
Bring milk to the boil and beat into the mixture. Return to the
saucepan, bring to the boil and simmer for 2 minutes. Remove
from the heat. Stir in essence and remaining Vermouth.

3 Whisk egg whites until stiff, add remaining sugar
and whisk until glossy. Fold into Vermouth mixture.
Spoon into grapefruit cups and bake at 200°C (400°F),
mark 6 for 5 minutes. Dust tops with sifted icing
sugar and return to oven for 2 minutes.
Serve with the grapefruit sauce.

240 Calories per portion

Raspberry Clafoutis SERVES 4

Butter - *10g (⅓ oz) approx.*
Eggs - *3 (size 3)*
Caster sugar - *50g (2oz)*

Plain flour - *50g (2oz)*
Fresh milk - *300ml (½ pint)*
Raspberries - *225g (8oz)*

METHOD

1 Lightly grease an ovenproof dish with butter.

2 Whisk eggs and sugar until pale and frothy. Stir in flour then milk. Pour half batter into the dish. Bake at 200°C (400°F), mark 6 for 15 minutes.

3 Arrange raspberries on top of batter, pour remaining batter around the fruit. Return to the oven for 30 minutes until golden. Serve hot sprinkled with a little extra sugar.

260 Calories per portion **F**

Thai Custard SERVES 6

Fresh milk - *350ml (12 fl oz)*
Desiccated coconut - *100g (4oz)*
Semolina - *50g (2oz)*
Eggs - *3 (size 3) beaten*

Caster sugar - *75g (3oz)*
Kiwi fruit - *2*
Star fruit - *1*

METHOD

1 Place milk in a saucepan. Bring to the boil, add coconut, pour into a basin and leave to cool.

2 Beat semolina, eggs and sugar into the cooled milk. Place basin over a pan of simmering water and stir until the mixture thickens.

3 Pour into a greased 900g (2lb) loaf tin and bake at 180°C (350°F), mark 4 for 30 minutes. Grill under a pre-heated grill until golden. Cut into bars and serve warm with slices of kiwi and star fruit.

425 Calories per portion Ⓕ

Raspberry Ice SERVES 4

Raspberries - *225g (8oz)*
Eggs - *2 (size 3) beaten*
Fresh milk - *450ml (¾ pint)*
Caster sugar - *100g (4oz)*
Fresh double cream - *150ml (¼ pint)*
Low fat raspberry yogurt - *150g (5oz)*

METHOD

1 Sieve 175g (6oz) raspberries.

2 Beat eggs, milk and sugar in a basin over a saucepan of simmering water, stirring continuously until mixture coats the back of spoon.

3 Cool the custard. Stir in cream, yogurt and raspberry purée. Pour into freezer tray and freeze until almost solid.

4 Transfer to a basin and whisk until smooth. Fold in whole raspberries. Return to freezer tray. Freeze until firm. Place in refrigerator for 30 minutes before serving.

420 Calories per portion Ⓕ

Summer Fruit Ice Cream SERVES 6

Mixed summer fruits
    (redcurrants, blackcurrants, raspberries) - *450g (1 lb)*
Caster sugar - *100g (4oz)*
Lemon juice - *5ml (1 tsp)*
Fresh double cream - *450ml (¾ pint)*
Fresh mint - *for decoration*

METHOD

1 Place fruits, sugar, lemon juice and 150ml (¼ pint) water in a saucepan. Simmer for 6 minutes. Cool then sieve to remove seeds.

2 Whip cream until it just holds its shape on the whisk. Fold in the purée, pour into a container and freeze. Beat mixture twice at hourly intervals then cover, seal and freeze. Place in the refrigerator for 30 minutes before serving decorated with mint.

180 Calories per portion Ⓕ

Iced Mocha Soufflé   SERVES 4

Plain chocolate - *25g (1 oz), melted*
Coffee granules - *10ml (2 tsp)*
Fresh milk - *150ml (¼ pint)*
Fresh double cream - *150ml (¼ pint)*
Egg white* - *1 (size 3)*
Caster sugar - *50g (2oz)*
*See page 2

METHOD

1 Melt chocolate and coffee granules together in a bowl. Heat milk to almost boiling and pour slowly onto chocolate, stirring all the time. Leave to cool.

2 Whip cream until it just holds its shape. Whisk egg white until stiff. Fold the sugar into the egg white followed by the cream.

3 Pour into a plastic box, cover and freeze for 4-6 hours until firm. Place in the refrigerator for 30 minutes to soften before serving.

---

405 Calories per portion Ⓕ

Christmas Pudding Ice Cream   SERVES 6

Mixed dried fruit - *100g (4oz)*
Dark rum - *60ml (4 tbsp)*
Port - *30ml (2 tbsp)*
Fresh single cream - *450ml (¾ pint)*
Egg yolks - *3 (size 3)*

Caster sugar - *100g (4oz)*
Fresh whipping cream - *150ml (¼ pint)*
Orange - *1, zest only*
Mixed spice - *5ml (1 tsp)*

METHOD

1 Mix dried fruit, rum and port. Leave for several hours.

2 Gently heat single cream to simmering point.

3 Beat yolks and sugar until pale and fluffy. Add hot cream, stirring continuously. Strain into a heavy based saucepan and stir over a gentle heat until the custard coats the back of the spoon. Cool by standing pan in a bowl of cold water and stirring custard continuously.

4 Whip cream until softly stiff. Fold into custard with fruit, zest and spice. Pour into a container and freeze. Beat mixture twice at hourly intervals then cover, seal and freeze.

230 Calories per portion

Dried Fruit Mousse SERVES 4

Dried apricots - *100g (4oz)*
Prunes - *50g (2oz)*
Orange juice - *225ml (8 fl oz)*
Gelatine - *11g sachet*
Fresh milk - *150ml (¼ pint)*
Eggs* - *2 (size 3) separated*
Greek style yogurt - *200g (7oz)*
*See page 2.

METHOD

1 Place dried fruits in a basin with orange juice. Leave to soak for 8 hours. Drain, reserving the juice in a cup.

2 Sprinkle gelatine over reserved juice. Stand in a pan of hot water until gelatine dissolves.

3 Purée fruit and milk in a liquidiser or blender. Place in a saucepan, beat in yolks and stir over a medium heat until the mixture thickens. Stir in the gelatine. Cool.

4 Whisk whites until just stiff and fold, with most of the yogurt, into the fruit. Pour into serving dishes and decorate with swirls of yogurt. Chill before serving.

225 Calories per portion

Blackcurrant Meringue SERVES 4

Fresh milk - *300ml (½ pint)*
White breadcrumbs - *75g (3oz)*
Eggs - *2 (size 3), separated*

Soft brown sugar - *50g (2oz)*
Black or redcurrants - *225g (8oz)*
Caster sugar - *25g (1 oz)*

METHOD

1 Heat milk. Pour over breadcrumbs.

2 Cream yolks and brown sugar until fluffy. Stir yolks and blackcurrants into breadcrumbs. Pour into a 568ml (1 pint) ovenproof dish. Stand in a roasting tin half filled with water and bake at 180°C (350°F), mark 4 for 40 minutes.

3 Whisk whites until stiff and fold in caster sugar. Spoon on top of the pudding, return to oven and bake until golden. Serve hot or cold.

400 Calories per portion

Mandarin & Ginger Russe SERVES 6

Orange jelly - *135g packet*
Egg* - *1 (size 3), separated*
Caster sugar - *25g (1 oz)*
Low fat cottage cheese - *100g (4oz)*

Ground ginger - *5ml (1 tsp)*
Fresh double cream - *150ml (¼ pint), whipped*
Mandarin oranges - *298g can, drained*
Langue de chat biscuits - *24*
*See page 2.

METHOD

1 Dissolve jelly in 150ml (¼ pint) boiling water. Pour 1cm (½ inch) into base of 568ml (1 pint) soufflé dish. Allow to set. Cool but do not allow remaining jelly to set.

2 Cream yolk and sugar until fluffy. Stir in cottage cheese, ginger, remaining jelly, most of the cream and mandarins.

3 Stiffly whisk egg white and fold into mixture.

4 Arrange biscuits around edge of dish. When orange mixture is on the point of setting, spoon into the dish. Chill until firm.

5 Trim biscuits to the level of the top of the dish. Stand dish in hot water for a few seconds then turn onto a plate. Decorate with remaining mandarins and cream.

310 Calories per portion

Highland Treat SERVES 6

Butter - *50g (2oz)*
Plain flour - *100g (4oz) sieved*
Cornflour - *30ml (2 tbsp)*
Caster sugar - *10ml (2 tsp)*
Fresh milk - *300ml (½ pint)*
Whisky liqueur - *30-45ml (2-3 tbsp)*
Mincemeat - *175g (6oz)*
Fresh whipping cream - *75ml (5 tbsp), whipped*

METHOD

1 Rub butter into flour until the mixture resembles fine breadcrumbs. Mix to a dough with 30-45ml (2-3 tbsp) water. Roll out and use to line an 18cm (7 inch) flan ring. Bake blind at 200°C (400°F), mark 6 for 20 minutes.

2 Blend cornflour and sugar with a little milk. Heat remaining milk. Pour onto cornflour, stirring continuously. Return to the pan and bring to the boil. Cool sauce, by standing pan in a bowl of cold water and stirring continuously. Add liqueur, pour into flan case and leave to set.

3 Top with mincemeat and decorate with cream.

280 Calories per portion Ⓕ

Coffee Bavarois

SERVES 6

Coffee granules - *10ml (2 tsp)*
Coffee liqueur - *60-90ml (4-6 tbsp)*
Gelatine - *11g sachet*
Eggs* - *3 (size 3) separated*
Soft light brown sugar - *50g (2oz)*

Cornflour - *10ml (2 tsp)*
Fresh milk - *450ml (¾ pint)*
Fresh double cream - *150ml (¼ pint)*
Coffee beans - *to decorate*
*See page 2.

METHOD

1 Pour 45ml (3tbsp) boiling water onto coffee in a cup. Add liqueur. Stir in gelatine. Stand cup in pan of hot water until gelatine dissolves. Cool.

2 Whisk yolks and sugar in a basin until pale and fluffy.

3 Blend cornflour with a little milk. Heat remaining milk with 100ml (6tbsp) cream until almost boiling. Whisk milk and cornflour into egg mixture. Return to pan. Heat, stirring continuously, until mixture boils and is smooth. Cool slightly then add gelatine. Cool.

4 Whisk egg whites and fold into cooled mixture. Pour into serving dish. Chill. Whip remaining cream and decorate with cream and coffee beans.

435 Calories per portion

Coffee Cream Pie

SERVES 6

Shortcrust pastry - *175g (6oz)*
Coffee granules - *30ml (2 tbsp)*
Butter - *75g (3oz)*
Caster sugar - *75g (3oz)*
Egg - *1 (size 3)*
Fresh milk - *45ml (3 tbsp)*
Walnut pieces - *50g (2oz) finely chopped*

Plain flour - *75g (3oz), sifted*
Fresh soured cream - *150ml (¼ pint)*
Whole walnuts - *6, for decoration*

METHOD

1 Roll out pastry. Use to line 20.5cm (8 inch) flan dish.

2 Dissolve coffee in 15ml (1 tbsp) boiling water.

3 Cream butter and sugar until fluffy. Beat in egg. Fold in coffee, milk, chopped walnuts and flour.

4 Bake at 190°C (375°F), mark 5 for 35-40 minutes. Remove from oven, top with cream and walnuts. Serve hot or cold.

NB: Omit nuts if serving to young children.

315 Calories per portion Ⓕ

Coffee Creams

SERVES 4

Egg yolks - *3 (size 3)*
Caster sugar - *40g (1½ oz)*
Gelatine - *11g sachet*
Fresh milk - *300ml (½ pint)*
Medium ground coffee - *10ml (2 tsp)*
Fresh double cream - *150ml (¼ pint)*
Coffee beans - *to decorate*

METHOD

1 Whisk yolks and sugar in a bowl until whisk leaves a trail.

2 Sprinkle gelatine over 45ml (3tbsp) hot water. Stand cup in a pan of hot water and stir until dissolved.

3 Heat milk and coffee until almost boiling. Pour onto yolks, stirring continuously. Return to pan and heat, stirring, until mixture coats the back of the spoon. Sieve and sprinkle with a little caster sugar to prevent a skin forming. Cool.

4 Add gelatine and whipped cream to cooled custard. Pour into wetted moulds. Chill. Turn out and decorate with coffee beans.

---

360 Calories per portion Ⓕ

Belle Hélène Trifle

SERVES 6

Egg yolks - *3 (size 3)*
Caster sugar - *50g (2oz)*
Cocoa powder - *20ml (4 tsp)*
Fresh milk - *300ml (½ pint)*
Vanilla essence - *5ml (1 tsp)*
Fresh whipping cream - *150ml (¼ pint), whipped*
Dark rum - *45ml (3 tbsp)*
Trifle sponges - *8, halved*

Pear or black cherry jam - *30ml (2 tbsp)*
Pears in natural juice - *425g can, drained*
Chocolate dots and toasted almonds - *to decorate*

METHOD

1 Cream yolks, sugar and cocoa until fluffy.

2 Heat milk and essence. Pour, stirring continuously, onto egg mixture. Strain into a heavy based pan. Stir over a gentle heat until custard thickens. Cool. Fold in most of cream and the rum.

3 Spread sponges with jam. Arrange sponges and pears in the base of a serving dish. Moisten with a little pear juice. Cover with chocolate custard. Decorate with remaining cream, almonds and chocolate dots. Chill for several hours before serving.

155 Calories per portion

Chocolate Choux MAKES 15

Whole almonds - *50g (2oz) skinned*
Caster sugar - *50g (2oz)*
Butter - *50g (2oz)*
Plain flour - *65g (2½ oz)*
Eggs - *2 (size 3)*

Flaked almonds - *25g (1 oz)*
Custard powder - *15ml (1 tbsp)*
Fresh milk - *150ml (¼ pint)*
Plain chocolate - *75g (3oz), melted*
Fresh whipping cream - *100ml (4 fl oz) whipped*

METHOD

1 Make praline — slowly heat almonds and sugar in a saucepan until brown. Turn onto greased tin. Crush when set.

2 Heat 150ml (¼ pint) water and butter in a saucepan. When bubbling, remove from heat, tip in flour and beat until smooth. Cool. Beat in eggs, reserving 15ml (1tbsp).

3 Divide mixture into 15, spacing well out on a greased baking sheet. Brush with egg, sprinkle with flaked nuts and bake at 200°C (400°F), mark 6 for 10 minutes.
Cool on wire rack, slitting sides to allow steam to escape.

4 Make custard using powder and milk as directed on the packet. Cool. Add melted chocolate, cream and praline. Fill choux buns and serve remaining sauce separately.

315 Calories per portion

Chocolate Mousse Cups SERVES 6

Plain chocolate - *90g (3½ oz)*
Fresh milk - *45ml (3 tbsp)*
Fresh whipping cream - *200ml (7 fl oz)*
Chocolate cups - *6*
Strawberries - *100g (4oz)*

METHOD

1 Melt chocolate in a bowl over a saucepan of hot water.

2 Heat milk until boiling then whisk into chocolate. Leave to cool.

3 Slice strawberries. Reserve 6 and place remainder in chocolate cups.

4 Whip 150ml (¼ pint) cream until softly stiff. Fold into chocolate mixture. Spoon over the strawberries and smooth tops. Chill.

5 Whip remaining cream and serve cups decorated with cream and strawberry slices.

420 Calories per portion **Ⓕ**

Chocolate au Clare SERVES 4

Ratafia biscuits - *50g (2oz)*
Dark rum - *30ml (2 tbsp)*
Plain chocolate - *100g (4oz)*
Butter - *50g (2oz)*

Caster sugar - *50g (2oz)*
Egg - *1 (size 3), beaten*
Fresh milk - *150ml (¼ pint)*
Fresh single cream - *60ml (4 tbsp)*

METHOD

1 Soak ratafias in rum. Melt chocolate in a basin over a pan of hot water.

2 Cream butter and sugar until fluffy. Add melted chocolate.

3 Blend egg and milk in a saucepan and heat, stirring, over a gentle heat until mixture coats the back of the spoon. Stir into chocolate mixture. Leave to cool.

4 Divide half chocolate mixture between 4 serving dishes, cover with ratafias and remaining chocolate. Swirl a spoonful of cream through the chocolate using a skewer. Serve chilled.

---

350 Calories per portion **Ⓕ**

Chocolate Brandy SERVES 6

Plain chocolate - *175g (6oz)*
Eggs* - *3 (size 3), separated*
Brandy - *45ml (3 tbsp)*
Trifle sponges - *6*
Fresh whipping cream - *100ml (4 fl oz), whipped*
Cocoa and chocolate curls - *to decorate*
See page 2

METHOD

1 Melt chocolate over a pan of hot water. Cool.

2 Cream yolks and cooled chocolate. Stir in brandy.

3 Whisk egg whites until stiff. Gently fold 15ml (1tbsp) into the chocolate mixture then fold in the remainder.

4 Cut trifle sponges into three and cover the base of a glass bowl. Cover with a layer of chocolate mixture. Repeat the layers, finishing with chocolate. Chill for several hours. Serve decorated with whipped cream, cocoa and chocolate.

305 Calories per portion

Passion Fruit Mousse SERVES 4

Gelatine - *15ml (1 tbsp)*
Egg* - *1 (size 3) separated*
Caster sugar - *40g (1½ oz)*
Passion fruit juice - *300ml (½ pint)*

Fresh whipping cream - *225ml (8 fl oz)*
Chocolate hearts - *to decorate*
*See page 2.

METHOD

1 Sprinkle gelatine over 45ml (3tbsp) warm water in a cup. Stand cup in a saucepan of hot water until gelatine dissolves, stirring occasionally.

2 Whisk yolk and sugar in a bowl until pale and fluffy. Gradually whisk in fruit juice and cooled gelatine.

3 Whisk egg white until stiff. Gradually fold into the fruit mixture.

4 Whip cream until it just holds its shape. Fold three quarters into the fruit mixture, pour into 4 moulds and chill until set. Turn out and decorate with remaining cream and chocolate hearts.

---

145 Calories per portion

Passionate Hearts SERVES 4

Low fat soft cheese - *100g (4oz)*
Fresh double cream - *75ml (5 tbsp) whipped*
Passion fruit and peach yogurt - *50g (2oz)*
Caster sugar - *10ml (2 tsp)*
Egg white* - *1 (size 3) whisked*
Passion fruit - *2*
Shortbread hearts - *to serve*
Single cream - *to serve, optional*
*See page 2.

METHOD

1 Line 4 heart shaped moulds with muslin.

2 Blend soft cheese, whipped cream and yogurt. Fold in sugar and whisked egg white. Press into the moulds and stand on a wire rack over a plate. Refrigerate overnight to allow to drain.

3 Just before serving, turn hearts onto a plate and garnish with passion fruit. Serve with shortbread hearts and single cream.

290 Calories per portion

Fruit Fan

SERVES 4

Fresh double cream - *150ml (¼ pint)*
Egg white* - *1 (size 3)*
Orange brandy - *30ml (2 tbsp)*
Eating apple - *150g (5oz)*
Strawberries - *225g (8oz)*
Cherries - *175g (6oz)*
Apricots - *175g (6oz) halved*
Orange - *1, grated rind only*
*See page 2

METHOD

1 Place cream, egg white and brandy in a chilled bowl. Whip until softy stiff. Spoon into a bowl and chill.

2 Core and slice the apple. Dip in lemon juice if not serving immediately. Arrange apple and other fruits on individual plates. Serve with brandy cream, decorated with orange rind.

320 Calories per portion

Spiced Custard Slices

SERVES 4

Eggs - *2 (size 3)*
Sugar - *50g (2oz)*
Plain flour - *50g (2oz)*
Fresh milk - *300ml (½ pint)*
Fresh single cream - *225ml (8 fl oz)*
Ground cinnamon - *2.5ml (½ tsp)*
Lemon - *½, grated rind only*
Blackberries - *to serve*

METHOD

1 Beat eggs and sugar until pale and fluffy. Whisk in flour, milk, cream, cinnamon and lemon rind.

2 Pour into a greased, shallow ovenproof dish and bake at 180°C (350°F), mark 4 for 55-60 minutes until set. Allow to cool.

3 Serve chilled with poached blackberries.

265 Calories per portion

Hawaiian Delight SERVES 4

Fresh pineapple - *1 whole fruit*
Fresh fruit - *350g (12oz) selection of your choice*
Fresh double cream - *150ml (¼ pint)*
Icing sugar - *15ml (1 tbsp)*
Coconut rum liqueur - *15ml (1 tbsp) optional*
Pineapple yogurt - *75g (3oz)*

METHOD

1 Halve the pineapple lengthwise. Remove all the fruit to leave two shells.

2 Mix half the pineapple with the fruits of your choice.

3 Lightly whip the cream and sifted icing sugar, then fold in the liqueur and yogurt.

4 Fold the cream into the fruit mixture. Pile into pineapple cases and serve chilled.

The remaining pineapple can be eaten at breakfast time or to make a refreshing prawn cocktail.

320 Calories per portion

Italian Meringue SERVES 4

Cooking apple - *225g (8oz) peeled and sliced*
Blackcurrants - *100g (4oz)*
Blackcurrant jam - *20ml (4 tsp)*
Cannelloni tubes - *8*
Eggs - *2 (size 3) separated*
Cornflour - *5ml (1 tsp)*

Caster sugar - *50g (2oz) + 10ml (2 tsp)*
Fresh milk - *450ml (¾ pint)*
Lemon - *1, grated rind only*

METHOD

1 Poach apple and blackcurrants in 60ml (4tbsp) water until soft. Stir in jam. Cool.

2 Cook cannelloni in boiling water for 5 minutes. Drain, cool and fill with fruit mixture. Arrange in a deep, buttered ovenproof dish.

3 Beat yolks, cornflour and 10ml (2 tsp) sugar in a basin. Heat milk and lemon rind and whisk into cornflour mixture. Place over a pan of simmering water and stir until thickened. Pour over the cannelloni.

4 Whisk whites until stiff. Fold in remaining sugar and pipe meringue on top of cannelloni. Bake at 180°C (350°F), mark 4 for 30 minutes until golden. Serve immediately.

Cold Desserts

355 Calories per portion Ⓕ

Damson Cream

SERVES 4

Plums or damsons - *700g (1½ lb) stoned*
Red wine - *300ml (½ pint)*
Caster sugar - *50g (2oz)*
Eggs - *2 (size 3) beaten*
Ground almonds - *50g (2oz)*
Lemon - *1, juice only*
Fresh single cream - *150ml (¼ pint)*

METHOD

1 Poach most of the fruit in red wine until soft.
Drain and measure juice. Boil until reduced to
300ml (½ pint).

2 Liquidise fruit, juice, sugar and eggs. Heat gently,
stirring, until slightly thickened. Remove from heat,
add almonds and lemon juice. Pour into serving dishes
and chill. Serve topped with cream and decorate
with slices of plum.

---

260 Calories per portion

Swiss Roll Dessert

SERVES 6

Eggs - *3 (size 3)*
Caster sugar - *75g (3oz)*
Self-raising flour - *75g (3oz) sifted*
Strawberry jam - *45ml (3 tbsp)*

Thick custard - *300ml (½ pint)*
Fresh whipping cream - *60ml (4 tbsp)*
Low fat strawberry yogurt - *150g (5oz)*

METHOD

1 Grease and line a 30 × 20cm (12 × 8 inch) swiss roll tin.

2 Whisk eggs and sugar in a large bowl over a pan of hot
water until pale and thick — about 8 minutes.
Remove from heat and whisk a further 5 minutes.

3 Gently fold in flour, pour into tin and bake at
200°C (400°F), mark 6 for 10-12 minutes.

4 Turn onto a clean, dampened tea towel. Peel
off paper, trim edges, replace paper and roll up.
Leave to cool, covered with damp tea towel.
Unroll, spread with jam and roll up. Slice and
use to line a 568ml (1 pint) basin.

5 Mix custard, cream and yogurt, pour into
basin and refrigerate until set. Turn out of
basin before serving.

115 Calories per portion

Almond Floats

SERVES 4

Fresh milk - *300ml (½ pint)*
Sugar - *30ml (2 tbsp)*
Almond essence - *2.5ml (½ tsp)*
Gelatine - *11g sachet*
Tropical fruits (pineapple, mango) - *to serve*

METHOD

1 Heat 150ml (¼ pint) water in a saucepan with the milk, sugar and almond essence. Remove from heat. Cool.

2 Place 150ml (¼ pint) warm water in a basin. Sprinkle over gelatine and stand basin over a pan of hot water, stirring occasionally until dissolved. Add to milk mixture, pour into a shallow dish and allow to set. Cut into rounds and serve with fruit slices.

380 Calories per portion

Honeycomb Flan

SERVES 6

Egg* - *1 (size 3) separated*
Light soft brown sugar - *40g (1½ oz)*
Fresh milk - *45ml (3 tbsp)*
Vanilla essence - *2.5ml (½ tsp)*
Digestive biscuits - *100g (4oz), crushed*
*See page 2.

Butter - *50g (2oz) melted*
Fresh whipping cream - *150ml (¼ pint), whipped*
Chocolate honeycomb bars - *2 × 20g (¾ oz)*
Walnut pieces - *25g (1 oz), chopped*
Grated chocolate - *15g (½ oz), grated*

METHOD

1 Blend yolk, sugar, milk and vanilla essence in a saucepan. Heat, stirring continuously, without boiling for about 10 minutes until mixture coats the back of the spoon. Put in a shallow, plastic container. Freeze for 1-1½ hours or until firm.

2 Mix biscuits and butter. Press in base and sides of 15cm (6 inch) flan tin. Chill.

3 Whisk egg white until stiff. Gently fold into whipped cream.

4 Slightly soften frozen mixture. Fold in chopped honeycomb bars, walnuts and cream. Pour onto biscuit base. Freeze until firm.

5 Place 4 triangles of greaseproof paper on top, leaving space between them. Sprinkle with chocolate, remove paper and serve frozen.

255 Calories per portion Ⓕ

Gooseberry Ring
SERVES 4

Fresh milk - *475ml (16 fl oz)*
Semolina - *50g (2oz)*
Caster sugar - *75g (3oz)*
Lemon - *1, grated rind only*
Eggs* - *2 (size 3) separated*
Gooseberries - *425g (14oz)*
*See page 2.

METHOD

1 Heat milk, sprinkle in semolina and simmer until thick. Add half the sugar and lemon rind. Cool and stir in egg yolks.

2 Simmer gooseberries and remaining sugar in a little water until tender. Reserve a few for decoration, purée the rest and fold into semolina.

3 Whisk egg whites until stiff and fold into semolina. Pour into wetted ring mould. Chill. Invert on to a serving plate and fill centre with remaining gooseberries.

150 Calories per portion

Melon Meringue Anise
SERVES 6

Light muscovado sugar - *75g (3oz)*
Egg whites - *3 (size 3)*
Cornflour - *20g (¾ oz)*
Fresh milk - *150ml (¼ pint)*

Low fat melon yogurt - *225g (8oz)*
Aniseed spirit - *30ml (2 tbsp)*
Melon - *1 small ripe, scooped into balls*

METHOD

1 Whisk whites until stiff. Whisk in ⅔ sugar. Fold in remainder. Fill piping bag. Pipe 8 rosettes and 2 × 20.5cm (8 inch) circles on oiled, greaseproof paper on a baking sheet. Bake at 110°C (225°F), mark ¼ for 1-1½ hours until crisp.

2 Blend cornflour with a little milk. Pour into saucepan with remaining milk. Heat gently, stirring, until mixture thickens. Cool by standing pan in cold water and stirring sauce. Stir in yogurt and alcohol.

3 Reserve 8 melon balls and arrange rest on meringue base with half sauce. Top with other meringue, remaining sauce, melon and rosettes.

285 Calories per portion

Orange Liqueur Mousse SERVES 4

Sugar - *25g (1 oz)*
Eggs* - *2 (size 3) separated*
Fresh milk - *300ml (½ pint)*
Orange liqueur - *30-45ml (2-3 tbsp)*

Gelatine - *11g sachet*
Oranges - *2*
Fresh whipping cream - *75ml (5 tbsp), whipped*
*See page 2.

METHOD

1 Beat sugar, yolks, milk and liqueur until smooth.

2 Sprinkle gelatine over 45ml (3tbsp) warm water in cup. Stand cup in saucepan of hot water and stir until gelatine dissolves. Add to milk. Cool. Softly whisk whites and fold into mixture.

3 Peel and segment oranges, using a serrated knife to remove pith and dividing membranes. Arrange most segments in base of 4 glasses. Pour on the mousse. Chill until set. Serve decorated with whipped cream and orange segments.

320 Calories per portion

Hogmanay Syllabub

Medium oatmeal - *25g (1 oz)*   SERVES 6
Whisky - *60ml (4 tbsp)*
Lemon juice - *60ml (4 tbsp)*
Egg white* - *1 (size 3)*
Fresh whipping cream - *300ml (½ pint)*
Fresh milk - *30-45ml (2-3 tbsp)*
Chocolate flake bars - *3*
*See page 2.

METHOD

1 Soak oatmeal in whisky and lemon juice in a saucepan for 5 minutes. Then heat, stirring continuously, until it thickens. Cool.

2 Whisk egg white and cream until softly stiff. Gently fold in oatmeal and milk. Crumble two flakes and fold into mixture. Spoon into serving dishes and chill. Serve decorated with remaining flake.

345 Calories per portion

Whisky and Oatmeal Syllabub SERVES 4

Fresh whipping cream - *300ml (½ pint)*
Golden syrup - *15ml (1 tbsp)*
Whisky - *45ml (3 tbsp)*
Lemon juice - *5ml (1 tsp)*
Medium oatmeal - *25g (1 oz) toasted*

METHOD
1 Whip cream until softly stiff.

2 Mix together the syrup, whisky and lemon juice in a large bowl.
Gently fold in the cream and most of the toasted oatmeal.
Pile into glasses, chill well and serve sprinkled with
remaining oatmeal.

405 Calories per portion

Wine Jelly Cream SERVES 4

Dry white wine - *300ml (½ pint)*
Sugar - *45ml (3 tbsp)*
Brandy - *30ml (2 tbsp)*
Gelatine - *11g sachet*
Egg yolks - *2 (size 3)*
Cornflour - *15ml (1 tbsp)*
Vanilla essence - *5ml (1 tsp)*
Fresh milk - *568ml (1 pint)*
Fresh double cream - *150ml (¼ pint)*

METHOD
1 Warm half wine, 30ml (2tbsp) sugar and brandy in
a saucepan. Sprinkle over gelatine, remove from heat
and stir until gelatine dissolves. Add remaining wine.
Cool and pour into 4 glasses. Place in refrigerator
at 45° angle, to set.

2 Blend yolks, cornflour, remaining sugar and
essence. Bring milk almost to boil, pour onto
cornflour, stirring continuously. Return to
pan and simmer until thickened. Allow to cool.

3 Whip cream until softly stiff. Fold into custard.
Pour onto set jelly and return to refrigerator to chill.

415 Calories per portion

Pear and Hazelnut Meringue SERVES 8

Egg whites - *4 (size 3)*
Caster sugar - *275g (10oz)*
Vanilla essence - *few drops*
Vinegar - *5ml (1 tsp)*

Ground hazelnuts - *100g (4oz) toasted*
Conference pears - *450g (1 lb) peeled, cored and sliced*
Fresh double cream - *300ml (½ pint)*
Whole hazelnuts - *to decorate*

METHOD

1 Grease and line 2 × 20.5cm (8 inch) sandwich tins.

2 Whisk whites until stiff. Whisk in 250g (9oz) sugar, a tablespoon at a time. Continue whisking until meringue is very stiff. Fold in essence, vinegar and hazelnuts. Divides between the tins. Bake at 180°C (350°F), mark 4 for 45 minutes.

3 Place pears, remaining sugar and 15ml (1tbsp) water in a saucepan. Cover and simmer gently until just tender. Cool.

4 Whip cream until softly stiff. Fold well drained pears into two thirds of cream. Use to sandwich meringues together. Serve decorated with remaining cream and whole hazelnuts.

NB: Do not decorate with whole hazelnuts if serving to young children.

315 Calories per portion

Chestnut Meringue SERVES 6

Egg whites - *3 (size 3)*
Caster sugar - *115g (4½ oz)*
Fresh double cream - *150ml (¼ pint)*
Fresh milk - *15ml (1 tbsp)*
Dark rum - *45ml (3 tbsp)*
Sweetened chestnut purée - *250g (9oz) can*
Chocolate - *for decoration*

METHOD

1 Line 3 baking sheets with greased greaseproof paper. Mark 15cm (6 inch) circles on each.

2 Whisk egg whites until stiff. Whisk in half the sugar. Fold in remainder with a metal spoon. Spoon equal amounts onto each baking sheet and spread evenly to fill circles.

3 Bake at 130°C (250°F), mark ½ for 2½- 3 hours. To prevent cracking, allow to cool before peeling off paper.

4 Whisk cream and milk together until softly stiff. Gently fold cream and rum into chestnut purée. Sandwich meringues together just before serving. Decorate with chocolate shavings.

380 Calories per portion Ⓕ

Nectarine Cheesecake SERVES 8

Butter - *50g (2oz)*
Petit beurre biscuits - *150g (5oz) crushed*
Nectarines - *4*
Peach jelly - *135g (4¾ oz) packet*
Full fat soft cheese - *350g (12oz)*
Fresh whipping cream - *150ml (¼ pint), whipped*
Sprigs of mint - *to decorate*

METHOD

1 Melt butter in a saucepan. Stir in crumbs. Press into base of 20.5cm (8 inch) loose-bottomed cake tin. Chill until firm.

2 Peel 2 nectarines, remove stones and dice.

3 Dissolve jelly in 150ml (¼ pint) hot water. Gradually beat in cheese. Gently fold in cream and diced nectarines. Pour into tin. Chill. Remove from tin. Stone and slice remaining nectarines. Decorate with nectarine slices and mint.

270 Calories per portion Ⓕ

Cranberry Cheesecake SERVES 6

Butter - *40g (1½ oz)*
Wheatmeal biscuits - *100g (4oz) crushed*
Gelatine - *15ml (1 tbsp)*
Medium fat soft cheese - *100g (4oz)*
Caster sugar - *25g (1 oz)*

Low fat natural yogurt - *150g (5oz)*
Cranberry sauce - *200g (7oz)*
Fresh double cream - *150ml (¼ pint), whipped*
Egg* - *1 (size 3)*
Fresh cream and fresh cranberries - *to decorate*
See page 2.

METHOD

1 Melt butter in a saucepan. Stir in biscuit crumbs. Press into base of 18cm (7 inch) loose-bottomed cake tin. Chill.

2 Sprinkle gelatine over 30ml (2tbsp) warm water in a cup. Stand cup in pan of hot water. Stir until dissolved.

3 Beat soft cheese, sugar and yogurt. Fold in cranberry sauce, cream and gelatine. Whisk egg white until stiff. Gradually fold into the mixture. Pour onto biscuit base. Chill. Remove from tin and serve decorated with cream and cranberries.

370 Calories per portion

Lemon & Strawberry Cheesecake SERVES 6

Butter - *50g (2oz)*
Digestive biscuits - *150g (5oz) crushed*
Fresh double cream - *150ml (¼ pint)*
Lemon - *1, grated rind and juice*
Caster sugar - *50g (2oz)*
Cottage cheese - *225g (8oz)*
Fresh strawberries - *225g (8oz)*

METHOD

1 Melt the butter and stir in the crushed biscuits. Press into a 18cm (7 inch) flan ring.

2 Whip the cream until softly stiff. Fold in the lemon rind, juice, sugar and cottage cheese. Spread over the biscuit base and chill. Serve decorated with strawberries.

285 Calories per portion

Bavarian Cream Flan SERVES 6

Eggs - *2 (size 3) beaten*
Caster sugar - *65g (2½ oz)*
Fresh milk - *300ml (½ pint)*
Gelatine - *5ml (1 tsp) dissolved in 15ml (1 tbsp) water*
Vanilla essence - *few drops*
Fresh double cream - *150ml (¼ pint)*
Sponge flan case - *15cm (6 inch)*
Rhubarb - *2 sticks, sliced*
Strawberry jam - *15ml (1 tbsp) melted*

METHOD

1 Beat eggs and 50g (2oz) sugar, stir in milk. Heat in a saucepan, stirring continuously, until the custard thickens. Stir gelatine into custard. Strain and cool.

2 Fold essence and cream into the setting sauce. Pour into flan case.

3 Poach rhubarb in a little water with remaining sugar. Cool and drain. Arrange in centre of flan and brush with melted jam.

205 Calories per portion

Flummery Flan SERVES 4

Sponge flan case - *15cm (6 inch)*
Sweet sherry - *30ml (2 tbsp)*
Creamy fromage frais - *75g (3oz)*
Low fat fruit flavoured yogurt - *150g (5oz)*
Fresh whipping cream - *75ml (3 fl oz)*
Angelica and glacé cherries - *to decorate*

METHOD

1 Place the flan case on a serving plate and spoon over the sherry.

2 Beat together the fromage frais and yogurt. Whip the cream until softly stiff and fold into the yogurt mixture.

3 Spoon into the flan and decorate with angelica and cherries. Chill until ready to serve.

240 Calories per portion

Tropical Trifle SERVES 6

Jamaica ginger cake - *1*
Canned pineapple in natural juice - *225g (8oz) can*
Custard powder - *30ml (2 tbsp)*
Sugar - *25g (1 oz)*
Eggs - *2 (size 3) separated*
Fresh milk - *450ml (¾ pint)*
Caster sugar - *75g (3oz)*

METHOD

1 Slice the cake and arrange over the base of an ovenproof dish.

2 Drain the pineapple. Moisten cake using drained juice and cover with chopped pineapple.

3 Blend custard powder in a jug with the sugar, egg yolks and a little milk. Heat remaining milk until almost boiling. Stir into custard powder, then return to the saucepan. Cook for one minute, cool then pour into the dish.

4 Stiffly whisk the egg whites then gradually whisk in the caster sugar. Pipe a pineapple design onto the custard and place under a hot grill to brown.

370 Calories per portion

Devonshire Almond Dreams SERVES 4

Gelatine - *11g sachet*
Fresh milk - *225ml (8 fl oz)*
Devonshire cream liqueur - *45ml (3 tbsp)*
Almond flavoured liqueur - *30ml (2 tbsp)*
Sugar - *45ml (3 tbsp)*
Fresh double cream - *200ml (7 fl oz)*
Melted chocolate - *to decorate*

METHOD

1 Sprinkle gelatine over 75ml (5tbsp) warm water in a cup. Stand cup in hot water, stir until gelatine dissolves.

2 Blend milk, liqueurs, sugar and gelatine in a saucepan. Heating gently, bring to the boil. Simmer for 2-3 minutes until sugar has dissolved. Cool. Transfer to a bowl and chill for about 30 minutes until it starts to thicken.

3 Whip cream until softly stiff. Fold three quarters into chilled mixture. Pour into 4 glasses and chill for 4 hours. Serve decorated with remaining cream and chocolate.

---

380 Calories per portion 🄵

Gooseberry Tart SERVES 4

Butter - *40g (1½ oz)*
Wholemeal biscuits - *100g (4oz) crushed*
Ground cinnamon - *2.5ml (½ tsp)*
Cornflour - *25g (1 oz)*
Sugar - *50g (2oz)*
Vanilla essence - *2.5ml (½ tsp)*
Fresh milk - *450ml (¾ pint)*

Gooseberries - *225g (8oz)*
Nectarine - *1, stoned and sliced*
Quick setting gel - *1 packet*

METHOD

1 Melt butter in a saucepan. Stir in biscuits and spice. Press into base of 18cm (7 inch) flan dish.

2 Mix cornflour, half sugar and essence with a little milk. Bring remaining milk to the boil. Pour onto cornflour, return to pan and heat, stirring, until it boils and thickens. Cool and spread over biscuit base.

3 Cook gooseberries with remaining sugar until tender. Cool. Arrange gooseberries and nectarine over custard. Prepare gel as directed on packet and use to glaze tart. Serve chilled.

235 Calories per portion

Raspberry and Walnut Swirl

SERVES 4

Raspberries - *225g (8oz)*
Clear honey - *30ml (2 tbsp)*
Greek style yogurt - *225g (8oz)*
Very low fat fromage frais - *225g (8oz)*
Walnut pieces - *50g (2oz) roughly chopped*
Mint and raspberries - *to decorate*

METHOD

1 Lightly mash raspberries. Blend half the quantity of honey, yogurt and fromage frais then fold into raspberries. Spoon half the mixture into 4 glass dishes.

2 Mix remaining honey, yogurt and fromage frais with the walnuts. Spoon most of the mixture into the glasses. Top with raspberry mixture then remaining walnut mixture. Swirl two mixtures together and decorate with mint and raspberries.

NB: Omit nuts if serving to young children.

490 Calories per portion

Boozy Mallow Flan

SERVES 8

Butter - *75g (3oz)*
Digestive biscuits - *225g (8oz), crushed*
Marshmallows - *275g (10 oz)*
Fresh milk - *75ml (5 tbsp)*
Devonshire cream liqueur - *75ml (5 tbsp)*
Fresh whipping cream - *300ml (½ pint)*

MICROWAVE INSTRUCTIONS

1 Place butter in a 23cm (9 inch) flan dish. Cook on HIGH for 45 seconds until melted. Stir in biscuits. Press into base and sides of dish. Cook on HIGH for 1 minute. Cool.

2 Place marshmallows and milk in large bowl. Cook on HIGH for 3 minutes, stirring frequently, until melted. Cool. Stir in liqueur. Refrigerate for 1 hour until mixture thickens, stirring occasionally.

3 Whip cream until softly stiff. Fold three quarters into the mixture and pour onto biscuit base. Chill for at least 3 hours. Decorate with remaining cream.

Timings are for a 600 watt oven

450 Calories per portion

Brown Bread Cream with Damsons SERVES 4

Damsons - *225g (8oz)*
Caster sugar - *50g (2oz)*
Fresh milk - *450ml (¾ pint)*
Lemon - *1, grated rind and juice*
Eggs* - *3 (size 3) separated*

Gelatine - *11g sachet*
Wholemeal breadcrumbs - *175g (6oz)*
Fresh whipping cream - *150ml (¼ pint)*
*See page 2.

METHOD

1 Stew damsons until soft. Remove stones and add half the sugar. Purée in a food processor or blender.

2 Warm milk with lemon rind in a saucepan. Stand for 30 minutes. Cream yolks and remaining sugar until pale and thick. Pour over milk and return to saucepan. Heat, stirring, until thickened.

3 Sprinkle gelatine over lemon juice in a cup. Stand in a saucepan of hot water. Stir until dissolved. Add to custard. Cool then stir in breadcrumbs.

4 Whisk egg whites and cream together until softly stiff. Fold into custard. Pour into 900ml (1½ pint) mould and chill until set. Turn out onto serving plate. Serve with damson purée.

---

250 Calories per portion

Peggy's Pudding SERVES 4

Desiccated coconut - *15ml (1 tbsp)*
Fresh milk - *600ml (1 pint)*
Sago or tapioca - *50g (2oz)*

Caster sugar - *25ml (5 tsp)*
Cornflour - *15ml (1 tbsp)*
Brown sugar - *50g (2oz)*

METHOD

1 Soak coconut in 300ml (½ pint) warm milk for 30 minutes.

2 Gently simmer remaining milk, 300ml (½ pint) water and sago for 25 minutes until thick and creamy. Cool. Add 15ml (3tsp) sugar. Pour into 4 ramekins. Chill.

3 Blend sieved coconut milk with cornflour. Heat stirring until sauce boils and thickens. Add remaining sugar.

4 Melt brown sugar and 20ml (4tsp) water in a heavy based saucepan.

5 Turn out ramekins and serve with coconut sauce and melted sugar.

385 Calories per portion

Caramel and Banana Cups   SERVES 4

Light muscavado sugar - *50g (2oz)*
Fresh milk - *750ml (1¼ pints)*
Pudding rice - *100g (4oz)*
Vanilla essence - *5ml (1 tsp)*
Eggs* - *2 (size 3) separated*
Bananas - *3 × 150g (5oz)*
Lemon juice - *15ml (1 tbsp)*
*See page 2.

METHOD

1 Place sugar and 45ml (3 tbsp) water in a heavy
based saucepan. Heat gently until golden brown.
Remove from heat, plunge pan into bowl of cold water.

2 Add milk, rice and essence to sugar in pan. Bring
to the boil. Simmer until all milk has been absorbed. Beat
yolks into rice mixture. Cool.

3 Whisk whites until stiff and fold into mixture. Place a layer
of rice in 4 glass dishes. Cover with slices of banana dipped
in lemon juice. Reserving a few slices of banana for decoration,
repeat layers finishing with rice. Chill before serving.

---

395 Calories per portion

Caribbean Rice   SERVES 4

Raisins - *50g (2oz)*
Glacé cherries - *15g (½ oz)*
Dried mixed peel - *15g (½ oz)*
Fresh ginger - *1cm (½ inch), grated*
Medium sherry - *75ml (5 tbsp)*
Fresh milk - *900ml (1½ pint)*

Pudding rice - *50g (2oz)*
Sugar - *30ml (2 tbsp)*
Vanilla essence - *2.5ml (½ tsp)*
Fresh single cream - *150ml (¼ pint)*
Orange juice - *250ml (9 fl oz)*
Cornflour - *15ml (1 tbsp)*

METHOD

1 Soak fruit and ginger in the sherry.

2 Heat milk and rice in a saucepan. Simmer
gently for 45 minutes until thick. Stir in sugar
and essence. Cool then fold in cream. Chill.

3 Blend orange juice and cornflour in a saucepan.
Heat, stirring until sauce boils and is smooth.
Cool.

4 Spoon half rice in a glass dish. Cover with
orange sauce, most of the fruit and top with
remaining rice. Serve chilled, topped with
remaining fruit.

390 Calories per portion

Summer Rice Mould SERVES 6

Short grain rice - *25g (1 oz)*
Fresh milk - *568ml (1 pint)*
Ground nutmeg - *5ml (1 tsp)*
Sugar - *15ml (1 tbsp)*
Gelatine - *15ml (1 tbsp)*
Flaked almonds - *50g (2oz) toasted*
Fresh double cream - *300ml (½ pint)*
Peaches - *3, peeled and chopped*

METHOD

1 Place rice, milk, nutmeg and sugar in a saucepan.
Bring to the boil. Simmer gently for 30 minutes, stirring
occasionally. Cool.

2 Sprinkle gelatine over 30ml (2tbsp) warm water in a
cup. Stand in a pan of hot water, stirring occasionally
until dissolved.

3 Stir gelatine and almonds into cold rice mixture. Whip
cream until softly stiff and fold into mixture with the
peaches. Pour into greased 900ml (1½ pint) jelly mould.
Leave to set. Chill. To turn out, dip mould in hot water
for a few seconds then invert onto a plate.

360 Calories per portion

Peanut Velvet SERVES 4

Fresh milk - *568ml (1 pint)*
Crunchy peanut butter - *75g (3oz)*
Sago or tapioca - *50g (2oz)*
Sugar - *25g (1 oz)*
Low fat natural yogurt - *150g (5oz)*
Fresh whipping cream - *60ml (4 tbsp)*
Dry roasted peanuts - *to decorate*

METHOD

1 Gently heat milk. Pour gradually onto peanut butter,
stirring until well blended. Return to pan, add sago and
bring to the boil. Simmer gently for 20 minutes,
stirring frequently. Stir in sugar and cool.

2 Fold in yogurt, spoon into 4 dishes and chill.
Whip cream until softly stiff and pipe onto
desserts. Decorate with peanuts.

*NB: Do not add whole peanuts
if serving to young children.*

290 Calories per portion

Peachy Cheese Slice SERVES 7

Chewy cereal bars - *7*
Medium fat curd cheese - *350g (12oz)*
Icing sugar - *25g (1 oz)*
Low fat peach yogurt - *150g (5oz)*

Gelatine - *11g sachet*
Peaches in natural juice - *425g can, drained*
Egg white* - *1 (size 3)*
Lime - *1, sliced to decorate*
*See page 2

METHOD

1 Line a 900g (2lb) loaf tin with greaseproof paper. Place cereal bars across base, covering it completely.

2 Beat cheese, icing sugar and yogurt until smooth.

3 Sprinkle gelatine over 45ml (3tbsp) warm water in a cup. Stand in pan of hot water, stirring occasionally until dissolved.

4 Reserve 3 peach slices for decoration. Dice the rest. Fold peaches and gelatine into cheese mixture.

5 Whisk egg white until stiff. Fold into peach mixture. Pour into loaf tin. Chill until set. Turn out and decorate with peach and lime slices.

310 Calories per portion

Gooseberry Creams SERVES 4

Cornflour - *45ml (3 tbsp)*
Sugar - *25g (1 oz)*
Fresh milk - *225ml (8 fl oz)*
Butter - *15g (½ oz)*
Vanilla essence - *few drops*
Gooseberries - *225g (8oz)*

Icing sugar - *50g (2oz)*
Fresh whipping cream - *150ml (¼ pint)*
Lemon rind - *to decorate*

MICROWAVE INSTRUCTIONS

1 Mix cornflour, sugar, milk, butter and essence in a bowl. Cook on HIGH for 3½ minutes, stirring after 2 minutes. Stir well and cool.

2 Place gooseberries and icing sugar in a bowl. Cook on HIGH for 3 minutes. Purée in a food processor or blender. Fold into custard. Cool.

3 Whip cream until softly stiff. Fold into custard. Spoon into 4 glass dishes and chill. Decorate with lemon rind before serving.

Timings are for a 600 watt oven.

170 Calories per portion

Mango Fool SERVES 4

Mango - *1 large, approx 275g (10oz)*
Lemon juice - *15ml (1 tbsp)*

Egg white* - *1 (size 3)*
Fresh whipping cream
  - *150ml (¼ pint)*

*See page 2

METHOD

1 Peel and remove stone from mango. Purée two thirds in a food processor or blender. Chop remainder, stir in lemon juice and spoon into 4 glasses.

2 Whip egg white and cream until stiff. Fold in mango purée and spoon into glasses. Serve chilled.

485 Calories per portion

Yogurt Custard Tarts SERVES 4

Wholemeal pastry - *made from 175g (6oz) flour and 75g (3oz) butter*
Custard powder - *45ml (3 tbsp)*
Sugar - *15ml (1 tbsp)*
Fresh milk - *300ml (½ pint)*
Greek style natural yogurt - *150g (5oz)*
Selection of fresh fruit - *to decorate*

METHOD

1 Use pastry to line 4 × 10cm (4 inch) metal flan tins. Bake blind at 200°C (400°F), mark 6 for 20 minutes.

2 Blend custard powder and sugar with a little milk. Bring remaining milk to the boil. Pour onto the custard powder, stirring continuously. Return to pan and bring to the boil, stirring. Simmer for 2 minutes. Stand pan in a bowl of cold water, stirring custard until cool. Fold in yogurt.

3 Spoon custard into flan cases. Chill for 30 minutes. Serve decorated with fresh fruit.

320 Calories per portion

Lemon Zabaglione SERVES 4

Eggs - *3 (size 3)*
Caster sugar - *50g (2oz)*
Lemon - *1, grated rind only*

Dry Vermouth - *150ml (¼ pint)*
Fresh double cream - *150ml (¼ pint)*
Sponge fingers - *to serve*

METHOD

1 Whisk eggs, sugar and lemon rind in a bowl over a saucepan of simmering water until thick and foamy.

2 Add vermouth and cream. Continue whisking until thick. Pour into 4 wine glasses and serve with sponge fingers.

---

250 Calories per portion

Strawberry Flan SERVES 6

Plain flour - *150g (5oz)*
Butter - *50g (2oz)*
Fresh milk - *300ml (½ pint)*
Caster sugar - *25g (1 oz)*

Egg yolks - *2 (size 3)*
Fresh strawberries - *450g (1lb)*
Strawberry jam - *30-45ml (2-3 tbsp)*

METHOD

1 Place 100g (4oz) flour in a bowl. Rub in butter until mixture resembles fine breadcrumbs. Mix to a dough with 30ml (2tbsp) water. Roll out to line an 18cm (7 inch) metal flan ring. Bake blind at 200°C (400°F), mark 6 for 15 minutes. Cool.

2 Blend a little milk with remaining flour. Add sugar, whisk in yolks and remaining milk. Heat gently, stirring continuously, until custard thickens and boils. Cool.

3 Pour cooled custard into pastry case. Halve strawberries and arrange on top. Warm jam with 15ml (1tbsp) water, sieve and use to glaze strawberries. Serve with remaining strawberries and fresh cream.

260 Calories per portion

Party Blancmange

SERVES 4

Icing sugar - *75g (3oz)*
Cornflour - *75g (3oz)*
Fresh milk - *568ml (1 pint)*
Milkshake syrup - *30-45ml (2-3 tbsp)*

METHOD

1 Blend icing sugar and cornflour with a little milk. Bring remaining milk to the boil. Pour onto cornflour, return to saucepan and beat over a gentle heat until thick and glossy. Stir in milkshake syrup.

2 Cool slightly then pour into decorative jelly moulds. Serve chilled.

220 Calories per portion

Yogurt Fluff

SERVES 4

Gelatine - *11g sachet*
Lemon - *1, grated rind and juice*
Eggs* - *2 (size 3) separated*
*See page 2.

Caster sugar - *30ml (2 tbsp)*
Low fat lemon yogurt - *300g (10oz)*
Fresh whipping cream - *75ml (5 tbsp), whipped*

METHOD

1 Sprinkle gelatine over lemon juice in a cup. Stand cup in a pan of hot water, stirring occasionally until dissolved.

2 Place yolks and sugar in a bowl over a saucepan of simmering water. Whisk until mixture thickens. Stir in gelatine. Cool.

3 Fold yogurt into cooled mixture. Whisk whites until stiff and fold into yogurt mixture. Pour into serving dishes. Chill. Serve decorated with cream and lemon rind.

200 Calories per portion

Caramel Rice Pudding   SERVES 4

Fresh milk - *568ml (1 pint)*
Pudding rice - *50g (2oz)*
Sugar - *10ml (2 tsp)*
Caramel candy bar - *1 × 50g (2oz)*
Jelly diamonds and angelica - *to decorate*

METHOD

1 Place milk, rice and sugar in a saucepan. Bring to the boil, stirring. Cover and simmer for 30 minutes until rice is cooked, stirring occasionally.

2 Break up and stir in candy bar. Serve hot or cold, decorated as illustrated.

185 Calories per portion

Stripy Jelly   SERVES 6

Custard powder - *30ml (2 tbsp)*
Fresh milk - *300ml (½ pint)*
Strawberry jelly - *135g packet*
Fresh whipping cream - *75ml (5 tbsp) whipped*
Dolly mixtures - *to decorate*

METHOD

1 Blend custard powder and a little milk. Bring remaining milk to the boil. Pour onto custard powder, stirring well. Return to pan and bring to the boil, stirring. Cool.

2 Make up jelly as directed on the packet. Pour one third of jelly into a jug. Add the custard, stirring well.

3 Pour half remaining jelly into a 900ml (1½ pint) glass dish. Chill until set. Pour half the custard on top. Leave to set. Repeat layers using remaining jelly and custard. Chill. Decorate with whipped cream and sweets before serving.

395 Calories per portion

Apricot Ginger Shortbread SERVES 8

Plain flour - *175g (6oz)*
Ground rice - *50g (2oz)*
Soft brown sugar - *50g (2oz)*
Ground ginger - *15ml (3 tsp)*

Butter - *100g (4oz)*
Apricots in natural juice - *425g can*
Fresh double cream - *300ml (½ pint)*
Angelica - *to decorate*

METHOD

1 Mix first 4 ingredients in a bowl. Work in butter, using fingertips. Knead well.

2 Roll out a quarter of dough. Cut out 6 × 5cm (2 inch) circles. Place on baking sheet. Press out remaining dough to fit a 20.5cm (8 inch) flan ring. Prick with a fork. Bake at 180°C (350°F), mark 4 for 15 minutes for the biscuits, 35 minutes for the base. Cool.

3 Drain apricots. Reserve and slice 3 halves. Chop the remainder.

4 Whip cream until softly stiff. Place 90ml (6tbsp) in a piping bag. Stir chopped apricots into remainder and spread over base. Pipe with swirls of cream, arrange biscuits on the top. Decorate with apricots and angelica.

---

370 Calories per portion **F**

Apricot Soufflé SERVES 6

Eggs* - *4 (size 3) separated*
Caster sugar - *75g (3oz)*
Fresh milk - *450ml (¾ pint)*
Apricots - *175g (6oz) canned, puréed*
Gelatine - *11g sachet dissolved in 45ml (3 tbsp) hot water.*
Fresh whipping cream - *300ml (½ pint)*
Flaked almonds - *toasted, to decorate*
Fresh apricot - *1, skinned*
*See page 2.

METHOD

1 Prepare a 568ml (1 pint) soufflé dish with a paper collar 5cm (2 inches) above the rim of the dish.

2 Cream yolks and sugar in a bowl. Heat milk to boiling, whisk into egg mixture. Place bowl over a pan of simmering water. Stir until custard thickens. Cool. Stir apricot purée and gelatine into custard.

3 Whisk whites and two thirds of cream until softly stiff. Fold into custard. Pour into soufflé dish. Chill until firm. Remove paper collar. Whip remaining cream. Decorate with cream, almonds and fresh apricot.

265 Calories per portion Ⓕ

Pashka   SERVES 8

Medium fat curd cheese - *450g (1 lb)*
Caster sugar - *75g (3oz)*
Vanilla essence - *2.5ml (½ tsp)*
Fresh double cream - *75ml (5 tbsp)*
Blanched almonds - *50g (2oz) chopped*

Raisins - *50g (2oz)*
Glacé fruit - *50g (2oz)*
Stem ginger - *1 piece, chopped*
Glacé fruit, angelica, almonds - *to decorate*

METHOD

1 Line a 900ml (1½ pint) basin with a double thickness
of scalded muslin.

2 Beat first three ingredients until smooth. Lightly
whip cream. Fold into mixture with remaining
ingredients. Spoon into basin. Fold cloth over
the top. Cover with a saucer and place a weight
on top. Refrigerate overnight.

3 Remove weight, unfold cloth and invert pudding
onto a serving plate. Peel off cloth and decorate with
fruit and nuts.

NB: Do not add nuts if serving to young children.

505 Calories per 450ml (¾ pint) yogurt

Greek Style Yogurt   MAKES ABOUT 450ml (¾ PINT)

Fresh milk - *450ml (¾ pint)*
Fresh double cream - *45ml (3 tbsp)*
Greek style yogurt - *10ml (2 tsp)*

METHOD

1 Sterilise a saucepan, bowl, cup, spoons, thermometer
and vacuum flask using tablets available for sterilising
babies bottles.

2 Whisk together milk and cream. Place in a saucepan,
bring to the boil and simmer for 10 minutes. Cool to
43°C (109°F).

3 Blend yogurt with a little cooled milk. Stir in
remaining milk. Pour into flask, seal and leave for
6 hours. Turn out into basin, stand basin in cold
water and stir yogurt until cool. Cover basin and
refrigerate for 4 hours to thicken. It will keep up
to 3 days in the refrigerator.

*Note: for a thicker yogurt, pour yogurt into a colander lined with
sterilised muslin and leave to drain for 2 hours.*

405 Calories per portion

Pancake Parcels   SERVES 4

Plain flour - *100g (4oz)*
Icing sugar - *25g (1 oz)*
Egg - *1 (size 3)*
Fresh milk - *300ml (½ pint)*
Butter - *15g (½ oz)*
Orange juice - *45ml (3 tbsp)*

Mixed dried fruit - *50g (2oz)*
Lemon - *1, grated rind only*
Medium fat curd cheese - *275g (10oz)*
Icing sugar and orange rind - *to serve*

METHOD

1 Place flour and sugar in a bowl. Break in egg.
Gradually add milk, beating to form a smooth batter.

2 Heat a little butter in a 18cm (7 inch) non stick
frying pan. When hot, pour in 45ml (3tbsp) batter,
tilting to cover base. When pancake moves freely, turn
and cook until golden. Make 8 pancakes.

3 Heat orange juice, mixed fruit and rind until fruit is plump.
Cool then mix with curd cheese. Fill pancakes and wrap into small
parcels. Serve topped with icing sugar and orange rind.

330 Calories per portion

Easy Fruit Brûlée   SERVES 4

Mixed summer fruits - *350g (12oz)*
Fresh double cream - *200ml (7 fl oz)*
Low fat natural yogurt - *200g (7oz)*
Demerara sugar - *60ml (4 tbsp)*

METHOD

1 Reserve some fruit for decoration. Place remainder
in base of an ovenproof dish.

2 Whip cream until softly stiff.
Fold in yogurt and spread
over fruit. Chill for 2 hours.

3 Sprinkle with sugar. Place under a
pre-heated grill until sugar melts and
caramelises. Serve hot or chilled,
decorated with fruit.

205 Calories per meringue

Witches Meringues   MAKES 8

Egg whites - *3 (size 3)*
Pinch of salt
Soft brown sugar - *175g (6oz)*
Fresh double cream - *150ml (¼ pint) whipped*
Milk or plain chocolate - *50g (2oz)*

METHOD

1 Place whites and salt in a large bowl. Whisk until stiff. Add sugar gradually, whisking well with each addition.

2 Line 2 baking sheets with non stick paper. Spread half meringue into 8 cat shapes, half into 8 witches hat shapes. Bake at 130°C (250°F), mark ½ for 1½ hours. Switch trays around after 1 hour.

3 Cool on wire rack. Sandwich with whipped cream and decorate with melted chocolate just before serving.

250 Calories per portion

Spider's Web Trifle   SERVES 8

Chocolate swiss roll - *1, sliced*
Fruit cocktail in natural juice - *425g can*
Orange jelly - *135g packet*
Custard powder - *60ml (4 tbsp)*
Sugar - *30ml (2 tbsp)*
Fresh milk - *568ml (1 pint)*

Orange food colouring - *optional*
Chocolate - *25g (1 oz) melted*
Chocolate matchsticks
and buttons - *to decorate*

METHOD

1 Arrange swiss roll in base of glass dish. Drain fruit, reserving juice, and place on top of cake.

2 Dissolve jelly in 150ml (¼ pint) boiling water. Make up to 568ml (1 pint) with reserved juice and water. Pour over fruit. Leave to set.

3 Using custard powder, sugar and milk, make up custard as directed on the packet. Cool, add orange colouring if desired, then pour over trifle. Chill thoroughly.

4 Pipe circles on top of trifle with melted chocolate. Draw a skewer through the circles from the outside to the centre then pipe with chocolate. Position sweets to look like a spider.

Cakes

460 Calories per portion Ⓕ

Special Chocolate Cake   SERVES 8

Butter - *100g (4oz)*
Caster sugar - *175g (6oz)*
Eggs - *3 (size 3) beaten*
Cocoa - *50g (2oz)*
Self raising flour - *225g (8oz)*
Fresh milk - *225ml (8 fl oz)*

Fresh whipping cream - *225ml (8 fl oz) whipped*
Mandarins in natural juice - *425g can, drained*
Grated chocolate - *to decorate*

METHOD
1 Cream butter and sugar until light and fluffy. Gradually beat in eggs, adding a little flour if mixture starts to curdle.

2 Sift cocoa and flour. Gradually fold into mixture with milk. Pour into two 20.5cm (8 inch) greased sandwich tins. Bake at 180°C (350°F), mark 4 for 25 minutes. Cool in tins for 5 minutes then on a wire rack.

3 Sandwich cakes together with half the cream, topped with mandarins. Decorate with remaining cream and chocolate.

450 Calories per portion

Chocolate Truffle Cake   SERVES 12

Plain chocolate - *425g (15oz)*
Coffee granules - *10ml (2 tsp)*
Butter - *90g (3½ oz)*
Caster sugar - *150g (5oz)*
Eggs - *4 (size 3) separated*

Plain flour - *40g (1½ oz)*
Ground hazelnuts - *25g (1 oz) toasted*
Fresh double cream - *300ml (½ pint)*
Strawberries and fondant leaves - *to decorate*

METHOD
1 Melt 150g (5oz) chocolate in a bowl over a pan of hot water. Dissolve coffee in 30ml (2tbsp) boiling water.

2 Cream butter and sugar until pale and fluffy. Beat in melted chocolate, coffee and egg yolks. Whisk whites until stiff. Fold into mixture followed by flour and nuts. Pour into greased 20.5cm (8 inch) cake tin. Bake at 170°C (325°F), mark 3 for 1¼ hours. Cool in tin for 15 minutes then on a wire rack.

3 Heat cream in a small saucepan until gently bubbling. Remove from heat and break in remaining chocolate. Cover and leave until chocolate melts. Mix well and chill for about 1½ hours until firm enough to hold a peak.

4 Cover cake with chocolate and decorate with strawberries and fondant leaves.

40 Calories per portion

Passion Cake SERVES 8

Butter - *200g (7oz)*
Light brown sugar - *200g (7oz)*
Eggs - *3 (size 3)*
Wholemeal S. R. flour - *200g (7oz)*
Baking powder - *5ml (1 tsp)*
Carrot - *275g (10oz) grated*
Walnut pieces - *100g (4oz) roughly chopped*

Lemon - *1, zest and juice*
Medium fat curd cheese - *175g (6oz)*
Honey - *10ml (2 tsp)*

METHOD

Beat butter and sugar until fluffy. Beat in eggs with a little flour. Fold in remaining flour and baking powder. Stir in carrot, most of nuts, lemon rind and 15ml (1tbsp) juice.

2 Pour into greased 18cm (7 inch) cake tin. Bake at 180°C (350°F), mark 4 for 1½ hours. Cool in tin for 5 minutes then on a wire rack.

3 Beat cheese, honey and remaining lemon juice. Spread over top of cake and sprinkle with remaining walnuts.

50 Calories per portion

Strawberry Crown SERVES 6

Butter - *50g (2oz)*
Plain flour - *75g (3oz)*
Eggs - *2 (size 3) beaten*

Flaked almonds - *25g (1 oz)*
Cornflour - *25g (1 oz)*
Caster sugar - *25g (1 oz)*

Vanilla essence - *5ml (1 tsp)*
Fresh milk - *450ml (¾ pint)*
Strawberries - *225g (8oz)*

METHOD

1 Put 150ml (¼ pint) water and butter in a saucepan. When bubbling, remove from heat. Add flour all at once. Beat until smooth ball forms in centre of pan. Cool for 1 minute. Add eggs gradually, beating vigorously, to give a piping consistency. Save a little egg to glaze.

2 Fit piping bag with 12mm star nozzle. Fill with mixture. Pipe 20.5cm (8 inch) circle onto a baking sheet. Brush with remaining egg and sprinkle with almonds. Bake at 180°C (350°F), mark 4 for 40 minutes until firm. Pierce side with knife to allow steam to escape.

3 Mix cornflour, sugar, essence and a little milk. Heat remaining milk, pour onto cornflour, return to pan and heat, stirring, until custard thickens and boils. Cool.

4 Halve choux ring and sandwich together with custard. Fill centre with strawberries.

320 Calories per portion

Cherry Cake SERVES 8

Self-raising - *175g (6oz)*
Wholemeal S. R. flour - *175g (6oz)*
Sugar - *75g (3oz)*
Butter - *100g (4oz)*
Baking powder - *2.5ml (½ tsp)*
Egg - *1 (size 3) beaten*
Fresh milk - *200ml (7 fl oz)*
Cherry pie filling - *175g (6oz)*

METHOD

1 Sift flours into a bowl. Add sugar and rub in butter until mixture resembles fine breadcrumbs. Reserve one third of mixture.

2 To remaining mixture, stir in baking powder, egg and milk. Pour most of this mixture into a buttered 23cm (9 inch) spring form pan. Hollow out the centre, fill with pie filling and cover with remaining mixture.

3 Sprinkle reserved mixture over the top.
Bake at 180°C (350°F), mark 4 for 50 minutes.

---

280 Calories per portion **F**

Tutti-Frutti Cake SERVES 8

Butter - *100g (4oz)*
Soft brown sugar - *100g (4oz)*
Eggs - *2 (size 3) beaten*
Self-raising flour - *175g (6oz)*
Chopped glacé fruits - *75g (3oz)*
Low fat natural yogurt - *150g (5oz)*
Fresh milk - *45ml (3 tbsp)*
Bicarbonate of soda - *2.5ml (½ tsp)*
Grated nutmeg - *5ml (1 tsp)*
Glacé icing and cherries - *to decorate*

MICROWAVE INSTRUCTIONS

1 Cream butter and sugar until pale and fluffy. Gradually beat in eggs with a little flour. Stir in fruits, yogurt and milk.

2 Sift remaining flour, soda and nutmeg. Fold into mixture. Spoon into a greased and base lined pyrex or plastic 1.7 litre (3 pint) ring mold.

3 Cover with absorbent kitchen paper. Cook on HIGH for 10 minutes. Cool in mould for 5 minutes then on a wire rack. Decorate cooled cake with glacé icing and cherries. Serve as a cake or with custard.

Timings are for a 600 watt oven.

Cakes

Ginger Cake SERVES 8

Butter - *100g (4oz)*
Soft brown sugar - *100g (4oz)*
Egg - *1 (size 3) beaten*
Wholemeal S. R. flour - *50g (2oz)*
Self-raising flour - *50g (2oz)*
Baking powder - *5ml (1 tsp)*
Ground ginger - *5ml (1 tsp)*
Fresh milk - *175ml (6 fl oz)*
Oats - *50g (2oz)*

Crystallised ginger - *25g (1 oz) chopped*
Icing sugar - *100g (4oz)*
Lemon juice - *15-30ml (1-2 tbsp)*

METHOD

1. Cream butter and sugar until pale and fluffy. Gradually beat in egg. Sift flours, baking powder and ginger then fold into mixture with milk, oats and crystallised ginger.

2. Pour into greased 23cm (9 inch) ring mould. Bake at 180°C (350°F), mark 4 for 1 hour. Cool in tin.

3. Blend sifted icing sugar and lemon juice to give a thick, coating consistency. Turn out cake and coat with icing.

Raisin Parkin MAKES 12 PIECES

Plain flour - *175g (6oz)*
Medium oatmeal - *50g (2oz)*
Bicarbonate of soda - *7.5ml (1½ tsp)*
Ground ginger - *15ml (3 tsp)*
Raisins - *100g (4oz)*
Soft brown sugar - *75g (3oz)*
Butter - *75g (3oz)*

Golden syrup - *50g (2oz)*
Black treacle - *50g (2oz)*
Egg - *1 (size 3) beaten*
Fresh milk - *150ml (¼ pint)*
Icing sugar - *optional*

METHOD

1. Mix first 5 ingredients in a bowl.

2. Melt sugar, butter, syrup and treacle in a saucepan. Pour over flour, add egg and milk and mix well. Pour into a greased, lined 26.5 × 18cm (10½ × 7 inch) cake tin. Bake at 170°C (325°F), mark 3 for 1 hour until firm. Cool in the tin.

3. Store in an airtight tin for 2 days before serving cut in squares and dusted with icing sugar.

260 Calories per slice

Banana and Date Tea Loaf MAKES 12 SLICES

Stoned dates - *225g (8oz)*
Bicarbonate of soda - *5ml (1 tsp)*
Fresh milk - *300ml (½ pint)*
Butter - *100g (4oz)*
Wholemeal S. R. flour - *275g (10oz)*
Chopped hazelnuts - *75g (3oz)*
Bananas - *2 × 175g (6oz) mashed*
Egg - *1 (size 3) beaten*

METHOD

1 Place dates, soda and milk in a saucepan.
Heat to boiling, remove from heat and cool.

2 Rub butter into flour until mixture resembles
fine breadcrumbs. Add 50g (2oz) hazelnuts and stir
in bananas, egg, cooled milk and dates.

3 Spoon into greased 1.1kg (2½lb) loaf tin. Sprinkle with
remaining nuts. Bake at 180°C (350°F), mark 4 for 1-1¼ hours
until skewer comes out 'clean'. Cool in tin for 5 minutes
then on a wire rack.

NB: Do not add nuts if serving to young children.

---

130 Calories per portion

Stollen MAKES 24 SLICES

Strong plain flour - *500g (1lb)*
Butter - *25g (1 oz)*
Easybake yeast - *7g sachet*
Caster sugar - *65g (2½ oz)*

Salt - *pinch*
Lemon - *1, grated rind only*
Ground cardamom - *5ml (1 tsp)*
Ground mace - *5ml (1 tsp)*

Fresh milk - *225ml (8 fl oz)*
Egg - *1 (size 3) beaten*
Dark rum - *30ml (2 tbsp)*
Mixed dried fruit - *175g (6oz)*
Marzipan - *50g (2oz)*
Icing sugar - *to decorate*

METHOD

1 Sift flour into a bowl. Rub in butter. Add yeast, sugar, salt,
lemon rind and spices. Beat milk, egg and rum and heat
to 42°C (110°F). Add to flour and bind together.

2 Knead dough for 10 minutes. Return to the bowl,
cover with greased cling film and leave to prove in a
warm place for 30 minutes.

3 Knead dough again for 2 minutes, working in the
dried fruit. Divide in half and shape into rectangles
23 × 7.5cm (10 × 3 inches).

4 Shape marzipan into a 23cm (10 inches) roll. Place down
the centre of one rectangle. Fold dough over, seal edges and
putting sealed edge underneath, place on a greased baking sheet.
Place other rectangle close to it. Cover with greased cling film.
Leave to prove in a warm place for 45 minutes.

5 Bake at 190°C (375°F), mark 5 for 30 minutes.
When cold, decorate with sifted icing sugar.

20 Calories per slice Ⓕ

Apricot and Prune Teabread MAKES 12 SLICES

Granary flour - *275g (10oz)*
Baking powder - *12.5ml (2½ tsp)*
Mixed spice - *7.5ml (1½ tsp)*
Butter - *75g (3oz)*
Ready-to-eat prunes - *100g (4oz) chopped*
Unsalted peanuts - *75g (3oz) chopped*
Dried apricots - *100g (4oz) chopped*

Soft brown sugar - *75g (3oz)*
Fresh milk - *200ml (7 fl oz)*
Egg - *1 (size 3) beaten*

METHOD

Sift flour, baking powder and spice into a bowl. Rub in butter until mixture resembles fine readcrumbs.

Stir in prunes, peanuts, apricots and sugar. Add milk and egg. Mix well. Turn into greased 00g (2lb) loaf tin. Bake at 180°C (350°F), mark 4 or 1 hour until a skewer come out 'clean'. Cool in tin for 5 minutes then on a wire rack.

NB: Do not add nuts if serving to young children.

75 Calories per portion

Crumble Cheesecake Bars MAKES 9

Soft brown sugar - *75g (3oz)*
Wholemeal flour - *100g (4oz)*
Butter - *100g (4oz)*
Rolled oats - *100g (4oz)*
Medium fat curd cheese - *225g (8oz)*
Sugar - *50g (2oz)*
Egg - *1 (size 3)*
Orange - *1, grated rind and 30ml (2 tbsp) juice*

MICROWAVE INSTRUCTIONS

Place sugar, flour, butter and oats in a bowl. Rub in butter until mixture resembles breadcrumbs. Reserve a quarter for the topping.

Press remaining mixture into base of a 15cm (6 inch) square dish. Stand on an upturned saucer in the microwave and cook on MEDIUM for 5 minutes.

Beat remaining ingredients and spread over base. Cook on HIGH for 3 minutes. Sprinkle with crumb topping and cook on HIGH for 2 minutes. Cool then refrigerate. Serve cut into squares.

Timings are for a 600 watt oven.

Cakes

60 Calories per muffin Ⓕ

Bran Muffins

MAKES 20

Wheat bran - *50g (2oz)*
Fresh milk - *225ml (8 fl oz)*
Plain flour - *100g (4oz)*
Salt - *2.5ml (½ tsp)*
Baking powder - *15ml (1 tbsp)*
Butter - *50g (2oz)*
Caster sugar - *50g (2oz)*
Egg - *1 (size 3) beaten*

METHOD

1 Soak bran in milk for 10 minutes. Sift flour, salt and baking powder.

2 Cream butter and sugar until pale and fluffy. Beat in egg, milk and bran. Lightly fold in flour.

3 Grease deep patty tins and divide mixture to give 20 muffins. Bake at 200°C (400°F), mark 6 for 25 minutes. Serve warm with butter.

195 Calories per muffin Ⓕ

Cherry and Walnut Muffins

MAKES 12

Plain flour - *150g (5oz)*
Wholemeal flour - *150g (5oz)*
Salt - *2.5ml (½ tsp)*
Baking powder - *12.5ml (2½ tsp)*
Soft brown sugar - *50g (2oz)*

Glacé cherries - *75g (3oz) chopped*
Walnut pieces - *50g (2oz) chopped*
Egg - *1 (size 3)*
Fresh milk - *225ml (8 fl oz)*
Butter - *50g (2oz) melted*

METHOD

1 Sift flours, salt and baking powder, returning bran to the bowl. Add sugar, cherries and walnuts. Mix well.

2 Lightly whisk egg, milk and melted butter. Stir into dry ingredients and mix until evenly blended. Spoon into 12 greased muffin tins and bake at 200°C (400°F), mark 6 for 25 minutes. Cool in the tin for 5 minutes then on a wire rack. Serve warm.

450 Calories per scone 🅕

Granary Herb Scones   MAKES 4 LARGE SCONES

Granary flour - *225g (8oz)*
Baking powder - *15ml (1 tbsp)*
Dried oregano - *2.5ml (½ tsp)*
Butter - *50g (2oz) + some for spreading*
Fresh milk - *150ml (¼ pint) approx.*
White Stilton with chives - *100g (4oz)*
Cucumber, tomatoes and lettuce - *to serve*

METHOD

1 Place flour, baking powder and oregano in a bowl. Rub in butter until mixture resembles fine breadcrumbs. Mix to a soft dough with milk.

2 Knead lightly. Roll out to approx. 1.5cm (¾ inch) thick. Cut out 4 × 7.5cm (3 inch) rounds. Place on a greased baking sheet, brush with milk and bake at 230°C (450°F), mark 8 for 10 minutes.

3 When cold, split and butter the scones. Fill with slices of cheese, cucumber, tomato and lettuce.

245 Calories per muffin 🅕

Chocolate Chip Muffins   MAKES 12

Self-raising flour - *225g (8oz)*
Wholemeal S. R. flour - *100g (4oz)*
Baking powder - *2.5ml (½ tsp)*
Banana - *1 × 175g (6oz) mashed*
Soft brown sugar - *75g (3oz)*
Eggs - *2 (size 3) beaten*
Fresh milk - *300ml (½ pint)*
Butter - *75g (3oz) melted*
Chocolate chips - *100g (4oz)*

METHOD

1 Sift flours and baking powder, returning bran to the bowl.

2 Mix banana and sugar until smooth. Add eggs, milk and melted butter. Stir into flours. Fold in chocolate chips.

3 Spoon into 12 greased muffin tins and bake at 200°C (400°F), mark 6 for 25 minutes. Cool in the tin for 5 minutes then on a wire rack. Serve warm.

290 Calories per portion Ⓕ

Lemon Buns MAKES 8

Strong plain flour - *350g (12oz)*
Salt - *5ml (1 tsp)*
Caster sugar - *75g (3oz)*
Ground cinnamon - *2.5ml (½ tsp)*
Ground cardamom - *2.5ml (½ tsp)*
Butter - *75g (3oz)*

Dried yeast - *10ml (2 tsp)*
Lemon - *1, grated rind only*
Fresh milk - *150ml (¼ pint) warmed*
Eggs - *2 (size 3) beaten for brushing*
Marmalade - *15ml (1 tbsp) warmed*

METHOD

1 Sift flour, salt, sugar and spices into a large bowl. Rub in butter. Stir in yeast and lemon rind. Beat in warm milk and most of the eggs to form a soft dough. Knead well. Place in a greased bowl. Cover with greased cling film and leave in a warm place until doubled in size.

2 Knead until smooth, divide and shape in 8 rolls. Cut a cross on top, place on a greased baking sheet, cover and leave until doubled in size.

3 Brush with beaten egg and bake at 200°C (400°F), mark 6 for 15-20 minutes until golden. Brush with marmalade. Serve warm.

570 Calories per bun Ⓕ

Greek Easter Buns MAKES 6

Butter - *50g (2oz)*
Fresh milk - *225ml (8 fl oz)*
Strong plain flour - *350g (12oz)*
Dried yeast - *7.5ml (1½ tsp)*
Soft brown sugar - *50g (2oz)*
Mixed spice - *7.5ml (1½ tsp)*

Hazelnuts - *100g (4oz) chopped*
Egg - *1 (size 3) beaten*
Apricot jam - *15-30ml (1-2 tbsp)*
Food colouring - *to colour marzipan*
Marzipan - *175g (6oz)*

METHOD

1 Melt butter and add milk.

2 Mix flour, yeast, sugar, spice and half hazelnuts in a large bowl. Add milk and half the egg. Beat to a soft dough. Knead for 5 minutes.

3 Divide and shape into 6 × 10cm (4 inch) rounds. Hollow out and fill centres with greased 6.5cm (2½ inch) ramekins, half filled with water. Prove until doubled in size. Brush with remaining egg. Bake at 200°C (400°F), mark 6 for 10 minutes. Remove dishes and cook a further 5-10 minutes until golden.

4 Brush with apricot jam and sprinkle with remaining nuts. Knead a little colouring into marzipan. Roll into egg shapes. Place in nests.

NB: Do not add nuts if serving to young children.

190 Calories per portion

American Pancakes MAKES 8

Plain flour - *225g (8oz)*
Baking powder - *20ml (4 tsp)*
Caster sugar - *10ml (2 tsp)*
Salt - *5ml (1 tsp)*

Butter - *40g (1½ oz)*
Eggs - *2 (size 3)*
Fresh milk - *350ml (12 fl oz)*
Maple syrup and whipped cream - *to serve*

METHOD

1 Sift first 4 ingredients into a bowl.

2 Melt 25g (1oz) butter. Whisk in eggs and milk. Stir into dry ingredients and mix until evenly blended.

3 Melt remaining butter. Brush a heated non-stick frying pan with a little butter. When hot, pour in sufficient batter to give 12.5cm (5 inch) pancake, 0.5cm (¼ inch) thick. Cook until surface looks bubbly, turn and cook until golden. Make 8 pancakes. Serve immediately with syrup and whipped cream.

100 Calories per biscuit

Oatie Biscuits MAKES 30

Butter - *175g (6oz)*
Raw cane sugar - *150g (5oz)*
Egg - *1 (size 3)*
Fresh milk - *60ml (4 tbsp)*
Raisins - *25g (1 oz)*
Wholemeal S. R. flour - *275g (10oz)*
Rolled oats - *75g (3oz)*

METHOD

1 Cream butter and sugar until pale and fluffy. Beat in egg and milk. Add raisins.

2 Fold in flour to give a fairly stiff dough. Form into 30 balls and roll each one in oats.

3 Place on a greased baking sheet, flattening each ball slightly and allowing space for biscuits to spread. Bake at 180°C (350°F), mark 4 for 15-20 minutes until golden. Cool. Store in an airtight tin.

Each recipe serves 1

Bedtime Milk Drinks

HOT MOCHA *155 Calories*
Gently heat
Fresh milk - *200ml (7 fl oz)*
in a saucepan. Blend with
Drinking chocolate - *10ml (2 tsp)*
Coffee granules - *10ml (2 tsp)*
Return to pan and re-heat.
For a treat, add
a chocolate flake.

REAL HOT CHOCOLATE *335 Calories*
Place
Plain chocolate - *25g (1 oz), broken*
Ground nutmeg - *pinch*
Fresh milk - *200ml (7 fl oz)*
in a saucepan. Heat gently
until chocolate melts. Do not boil.
Serve topped with
Fresh double cream - *15ml (1 tbsp) whipped*
Grated chocolate.

EASTERN SPICED MILK *135 Calories*
Heat
Fresh milk - *200ml (7 fl oz)*
Ground nutmeg - *pinch*
Ground cardamom - *pinch*
in a saucepan.
Serve sprinkled with
a little extra spice.

Each recipe serves 4

Anytime Milk Drinks

SHERRY POSSET *160 Calories per glass*
Heat
Fresh milk - *568ml (1 pint)*
Sweet sherry - *150ml (¼ pint)*
Ground nutmeg - *pinch*
Demerara sugar - *15ml (1 tbsp)*
in a saucepan.
Serve sprinkled with
Grated lemon rind.

BREAKFAST REFRESHER *170 Calories per glass*
Blend
Chilled fresh milk - *568ml (1 pint)*
Orange juice - *175ml (6 fl oz)*
Greek style yogurt - *75g (3oz)*
Banana - *1 × 225g (8oz)*
in a liquidiser until frothy.
Serve sprinkled with
Drinking chocolate.

RICH ICED COFFEE *195 Calories per glass*
Blend
Black coffee - *568ml (1 pint)*
Dairy ice cream - *4 scoops*
Fresh milk - *300ml (½ pint)*
in a liquidiser for a few seconds.
Serve chilled, sprinkled with
Grated chocolate

Fruity Milk Drinks

DRINKING YOGURT *180 Calories per glass*
Blend together
Fresh milk - *300ml (½ pint)*
Low fat orange yogurt - *150g (5oz)*
Orange juice - *100ml (4 fl oz)*
in a liquidiser for a few seconds.
Serve chilled, topped with
Grated orange rind.

FRUIT SLUSH *175 Calories per glass*
Allow
Frozen raspberries - *200g (7oz)*
to stand at room temperature
for 10 minutes.
Blend with
Fresh milk - *300ml (½ pint)*
Low fat raspberry yogurt - *60ml (4 tbsp)*
Honey - *10ml (2 tsp)*
in a liquidiser until slushy.
Serve immediately.

NUTTY BANANA SHAKE *250 Calories per glass*
Blend together
Low fat hazelnut yogurt - *90ml (6 tbsp)*
Bananas - *2 × 100g (4oz) peeled*
Fresh milk - *450ml (¾ pint)*
in a liquidiser
until smooth.

Serve immediately,
topped with
Banana chips.

Sophisticated Milk Drinks

CARIBBEAN COCKTAIL *160 Calories per glass*
Blend
Fresh milk - *150ml (¼ pint)*
Grenadine liqueur - *10ml (2 tsp)*
Banana liqueur - *10ml (2 tsp)*
Melon liqueur - *10ml (2 tsp)*
White rum - *10ml (2 tsp)*
in a liquidiser for a few seconds.
Serve decorated with
Cocktail cherries and
Slices of banana.

RUMBA *130 Calories per glass*
Whisk together
Fresh milk - *300ml (½ pint)*
Strawberry instant dessert - *10ml (2 tsp)*
Rum essence - *10ml (2 tsp)*
Serve sprinkled with
Toasted desiccated coconut - *5ml (1 tsp)*

BERRY MILKSHAKE *170 Calories per glass*
Whisk together
Fresh milk - *300ml (½ pint)*
Raspberry yogurt - *150g (5 oz)*
until frothy.

CAFÉ NOISETTE *110 Calories per glass*
Dissolve
Coffee granules - *5ml (1 tsp)* in
Boiling water - *30ml (2 tbsp)*
Blend with
Chopped toasted hazelnuts - *15ml (1 tbsp)*
Fresh milk - *150ml (¼ pint)*
Serve decorated with
Fresh single cream - *15ml (1 tbsp) to decorate.*

123

Index

Index

Index